# BECOMING A BILINGUAL FAMILY

# BECOMING A
# BILINGUAL
# FAMILY

## Help Your Kids Learn Spanish
### (and Learn Spanish Yourself in the Process)

BY STEPHEN MARKS

AND JEFFREY MARKS

*University of Texas Press*

AUSTIN

Requests for permission to reproduce material from this work should be sent to:
    Permissions
    University of Texas Press
    P.O. Box 7819
    Austin, TX 78713-7819
    http://utpress/utexas.edu/about
        /book-permissions

⊗ The paper used in this book meets the minimum requirements of ANSI/ NISO Z39.48-1992 (R1997) (Permanence of Paper).

LIBRARY OF CONGRESS CATALOGING-IN-PUBLICATION DATA

Marks, Stephen G. (Stephen Gary), 1952–
    Becoming a bilingual family : help your kids learn Spanish (and learn Spanish yourself in the process) / by Stephen Marks and Jeffrey Marks. — 1st ed.
        p.    cm.
    Includes bibliographical references and index.
    ISBN 978-0-292-74363-2 (pbk. : alk. paper)
    1. Bilingualism in children.
    2. Parenting.    3. Children—Language.
    I. Marks, Jeffrey R. (Jeffery Robert), 1957–
    II. Title.
    P115.2.M37    2013
    420′.42610973—dc23          2012037681

doi:10.7560/743632

Illustrations courtesy of The Graphics Factory

We dedicate this book to our kids:

*Olivia, Alex, Claire, Adrian, and Saraí*

# CONTENTS

# BECOMING A BILINGUAL FAMILY

# THE
# JOURNEY
## TO
# BILINGUALISM

# WHAT THIS BOOK IS ABOUT . . .

# AND OTHER THOUGHTS

This is the tour guide and phrase book for the voyage of a lifetime, a voyage that you will be taking with your kids. It is a voyage to bilingualism and, more than that, a voyage to the cultures and the peoples that make up the Spanish-speaking world. It is a voyage that begins in your own backyard, for indeed millions of your *paisanos* (countrymen and women) are fluent speakers of Spanish.

We wrote this book for English-speaking parents who wish to raise their children to speak both English and Spanish. From our own experience in raising bilingual children, and from talking to many other parents, we have become convinced of four things: First, raising a child bilingually is one of the most valuable experiences in early childhood education. (More on this later.) Second, many parents recognize this value and would give the gift of bilingualism to their children if they only knew how. Third, most parents are interested in sharing this learning experience with their kids but do not know where to begin. (This included us.) Finally, traditional language instruction materials do not prepare parents to talk to their kids. Indeed, even parents who have studied a significant amount of Spanish find that they have neither the vocabulary nor the sentence structure for "kid talk."

Over the years many parents have approached us, some complete strangers on the street, to ask us how we have managed to raise our kids bilingually. As we have come to share our experiences with others and to reflect upon them ourselves, we have found ourselves giving advice that really boils down to two simple and related educational principles. The first is that *bilingual education for young children is simply a matter of creating a bilingual environment.* That is, language acquisition in young children is not at all about instructing children in the language. Rather, it has everything to do with creating an environment in which children are in contact with the language. Because children are gifted language learners, they do not need language classes. They only need a bilingual environment to attain proficiency. The next chapter in this book shows you how to create a bilingual environment in your home and in your child's life.

The second principle is that *you the parent are a very important part of that bilingual environment.* Your willingness to learn along with your children and speak Spanish to them, especially in the early years, will enhance their bilingual environment in two ways. First, it will give your children an additional source of Spanish, a bit more of the day in which they hear and speak the language. More importantly, however, the mere fact that *mami* or *papi* is speaking Spanish in the house provides a powerful role model for your children. The fact that you are interested in Spanish, that you find it fun and exciting, will be internalized by your children and will contribute to making language learning a lifelong love of theirs. This motivational aspect of your child's environment leads us to the one cardinal rule underlying this book:

---

*¡La regla más importante!*
*(The Most Important Rule!)*
**Speak to Your Kids in Spanish!**
(Even if incorrectly.)

---

This book is designed to give you the confidence to speak to your kids in Spanish. It provides you with the vocabulary and structures you will use daily. You will be learning along with your kids.

### WHY RAISE YOUR KIDS BILINGUALLY?

Most of the parents we meet are convinced of the benefits of raising children bilingually. Your interest in this book suggests that you have already considered the merits of this endeavor and are intrigued by the possibility. Occasionally, however, parents who do not understand why we would do such a thing ask us to justify our choice.

Part of the answer is the old notion that parents inflict upon their kids that which they wish their parents had inflicted upon them. (Yes, our kids take music lessons as well.) Like many people, we have a fascination with language. Yet language acquisition can be a trying proposition for adults. If only our parents had taught us a second language as children! In "Bilingual Babes: Teach Your Child a Second Language," Ilisa Cohen explains:

> Why are so many families jumping on the bilingual bandwagon? "In our increasingly global world, parents realize that their kids will benefit from knowing more than one language," says Nancy Rhodes, director of foreign-language education at the Center for Applied Linguistics, in Washington, DC. "There's definitely been a grassroots push for more bilingual education in preschools." Exposing your child to a second language will help him learn about other cultures. Research has shown that bilinguals tend to be more creative thinkers than those who speak one language, and one study suggests that their brain functions may stay sharper as they age.[1]

There are many reasons to raise children bilingually, including the following:

1. Knowing another language is an asset that will help our children survive and thrive in the world. The world is becoming more international every day, and those with language skills are more in demand and have a greater variety of prospects open to them. On average, bilingual speakers exceed their monolingual counterparts in earnings.

2. Learning two languages early on makes additional language acquisition in adulthood that much easier. Barbara Zurer Pearson, bilingualism expert and author of *Raising a Bilingual Child*, notes that children "acquire precocious *knowledge about knowledge*, a capacity called 'metalinguistic awareness,' which is one of the foundational skills for learning how to read and write. Metalinguistic awareness will also help children when they want or need to learn a third (or fourth or fifth) language."[2] Thus if your kids ever want to learn

---

1. Reprinted with permission from the August 2006 issue of *Parents* magazine, copyright 2006. http://www.parents.com/toddlers-preschoolers/development/language/teaching-second-language/.

2. Barbara Zurer Pearson, *Raising a Bilingual Child* (New York: Living Language, 2008), p. 14.

French, Italian, or Chinese, they will find it much easier if they already have experienced learning Spanish.

3. Recent studies have shown that learning another language as a child promotes cognitive development that carries over to other intellectual activities, such as mathematics and logical reasoning. Dr. Pearson summarizes the results of a study on "divergent thinking," noting that "bilinguals were able to generate three times more high-quality hypotheses for solving science problems than the monolingual students."[3] They also showed a distinct advantage in selective attention, focusing on a specific aspect of a task while suppressing others.[4] In a 2004 article titled "Being Bilingual Boosts Brain Power," Miranda Hitti summarizes the results of a recent study published in *Nature*: "People who are bilingual have an advantage over the rest of us, and not just in terms of communication skills. The bilingual brain develops more densely, giving it an advantage in various abilities and skills, according to new research."[5]

4. Studying languages promotes interest in and teaches about the world and its people. It is a history, culture, and geography lesson rolled into one.

5. Learning another language, and learning about the related cultures, promotes tolerance and understanding. "A bilingual is more likely to understand that his or her perspectives are just two out of many. This is the basis of greater tolerance," writes Dr. Pearson.[6] (The latest studies in the field of bilingualism are fascinating, and Pearson's *Raising a Bilingual Child* provides excellent insight into these discoveries.)

6. Learning another language will eventually open another beautiful world of literature to our children. Much of the world's greatest literature is written in Spanish, including, for example, Cervantes's *Don Quixote, One Hundred Years of Solitude* by Nobel laureate Gabriel García Márquez, and the poems of fellow laureate Pablo Neruda.

7. Learning another language creates self-esteem. Our kids are very proud that they speak two languages. They recognize it as something special and powerful.

8. Learning another language creates opportunities for travel and exploration. (So far, we have spent summers in Mexico, Spain, and Costa Rica and have traveled to Argentina, Chile, and Ecuador.)

9. Learning a language is an intellectual activity that you truly can share with your kids (and one in which they may learn better and faster than you).

---

3. Ibid., p. 23.

4. Ibid., pp. 24–25.

5. http://www.webmd.com/parenting/news/20041013/being-bilingual-boosts-brain-power.

6. Pearson, p. 31.

10. Learning a second language is fun. It is fun for you and fun for your child. Learning along with your child will keep you in the mix on a daily basis. You will be practicing your Spanish throughout the day. Since parent-child interaction is intensive by nature, you will probably be getting more speaking experience than you would if you were vacationing in Spain or Mexico.

Finally, it should be noted that though many believe monolingualism to be the norm—based, no doubt, on their local experience—it is actually the exception. More than half of the world's population speaks two or more languages. In "A Global Perspective on Bilingualism and Bilingual Education" (1999), G. Richard Tucker notes that

> . . . there are many more bilingual or multilingual individuals in the world than there are monolingual. In addition, there are many more children throughout the world who have been and continue to be educated through a second or a later-acquired language, at least for some portion of their formal education, than there are children educated exclusively via the first language.[7]

For those parents interested in going deeper into the research on bilingualism and bilingual education, we have included a recommended reading list of books and articles and have provided some websites of interest at the end of the book.

### ARE THERE ANY NEGATIVES?

Some parents worry that learning Spanish may slow the development of English, which is admittedly the most important language to acquire for someone living in an English-speaking country. Researchers have studied the effects of bilingualism on the development of a variety of language skills. These studies are complex because of the  multitude of factors that need to be taken into consideration. For this reason, outcomes from these studies have varied somewhat. The bulk of the evidence, however, suggests that bilingual children develop linguistically as fast as, or faster than, their monolingual counterparts.[8]

---

7. http://www.cal.org/resources/digest/digestglobal.html.
8. See Pearson, chapter 7, for a detailed discussion of this research.

Granted, it takes a certain amount of interest and initiative to create a bilingual environment in your home. This book is designed to make that project easy and enjoyable. The next chapter discusses how to go about creating a bilingual environment for your child. Part II of this book is designed to make it easy for you to contribute to that environment directly, while working on your own language skills, by talking to your children. When we started speaking Spanish to our kids, we had to figure all of this out ourselves. This book will give you the benefit of our experience so that you have everything at your fingertips.

## WHEN TO BEGIN?

Babies are well equipped for language learning from birth. They are, in essence, little language-acquiring machines. The Multilingual Children's Association puts it this way:

> You could say the brain is "primed" the first three years of life with synapses at a peak, busily setting up the optimal neural pathways to mediate language. This construction of the brain's language chip continues, but at an ever-slowing rate until late childhood. Even if you don't start from birth, the earlier is truly easier for both you and your child. By the early teens, the baby's special abilities are completely gone. Besides, the younger the child, the less likely they will care about blatant errors. They'll just happily chatter away until your ears are ready to fall off. What better learning conditions can you ask for?[9]

Many bilingual children learn both languages from the very beginning. They essentially have two "first" languages. It is also common, though, for bilingual children to acquire a second language after their first language is well established. Each of these scenarios is effective, though they have different advantages and disadvantages on a cognitive level. It should be kept in mind, however, that there is a window, through puberty, during which children learn language with the greatest ease. There is now some physiological evidence confirming this, although why this window gradually closes in early adulthood remains a mystery. A recent study compared the brain activity of two sets of fluently bilingual adults. The researchers discovered that those who learned both languages as young children used the same part of

---

9. http://www.multilingualchildren.org/getting_started/tensteps.html

the brain for both languages. Those who learned the second language at a later age used a different part of the brain for each language.[10]

By no means should it be interpreted that older children and adults are incapable of achieving near-native proficiency in a second language. Nothing could be further from the truth. In fact, older children and adults have some advantages over young children. Because of their greater experience, both in the world and in their first language, older children and adults will be able to master more complex structures and achieve more nuanced meaning through applied study. Using the rules of grammar, which younger children are not likely to understand, they can make fast progress in a second language. It is true, however, that people who learn a second language after puberty are more likely to have a noticeable accent than those who acquire their second language earlier.

So the answer to the question of when to begin is *the sooner the better*—but you can't start any sooner than now.

## WHY SPANISH?

The language we chose was Spanish. Of course, this will not be everyone's choice. Some couples are bilingual, and for these the choice of the two languages may be quite natural. One parent may be a native English speaker, for example, and the other a native French speaker. In this case, raising the children in an English-French environment would be logical.

In the case of Mary and Steve, neither had any special competence in a second language. They chose Spanish for a variety of reasons. First, it is widely spoken. Second, Spanish is relatively easy to learn: pronunciation is straightforward; the alphabet is the same (with the exception of the ñ); the vocabulary, being Latin-based, has something in common with English; and the grammar is manageable. Third, they have access to abundant resources in Spanish, including books, videos, audio CDs, and computer programs. Many people in their community speak Spanish, and one often hears it on the street in their Boston area neighborhood. Finally, they have always loved Spanish and Latin American literature, even in translation. Thus, for Mary and Steve, Spanish was a natural choice. For Jeff's family, the choice was even easier: both parents are Spanish and English speakers.

---

10. "The Bilingual Brain," *Discover*, Oct. 1997. http://discovermagazine.com/1997/oct /thebilingualbrai1258/.

## EDUCATING MOM AND DAD

Once you decide to raise your kids bilingually, you will probably want to study Spanish yourself or brush up on that Spanish that you learned way back in high school or college (it does come back to you!). In the chapter *Grammar Enough to Get You Started*, we give you a fairly complete guide to basic Spanish grammar so that you will need only one book close at hand. *Becoming a Bilingual Family* is not intended as a complete course of study, however. Here, we have organized the material thematically so that you can easily find what you want to say, whether you are getting your toddler ready for the playground or discussing your ten-year-old's soccer game. Spanish courses for adults organize their material by grammatical concepts that your children will not know, nor need to know, as they acquire the language through contact with it in their daily environment. From an adult perspective, then, this book should be considered a supplement to formal study. You may want to take some courses at the local college or through an adult education program. Or, perhaps, you will want to buy instructional books or CDs. We learned this way, primarily through books and CDs. (The commute to work, if you have one, is a great place to learn a language.) A wealth of well-designed materials is out there to make home study effective and enjoyable.

You will find, however, that these classes, books, and CDs will leave you still stumbling when it comes to speaking with your kids because these materials are directed at adults. The dialogues and vocabulary generally focus on businesspeople, university students, and travelers. We are not aware of any other book that provides the vocabulary and sentence structure for talking to kids. Even those parents who have studied Spanish for a number of years often have no idea about how to ask a child if she has to go to the bathroom, if she wants to play hide-and-seek, if she has a dirty diaper, if she wants to be pushed on the swings, or if something hurts. This book fills that

gap. It supplements your adult language study in that it extends your vocabulary and, most importantly, assures that every day you are putting into practice the Spanish you are learning. You have a captive, attentive, and loving audience for your practice!

## HOW THIS BOOK CAME ABOUT

Over the years we have interacted with a multitude of parents who were in the process of bringing up their kids bilingually. We might find ourselves on a park bench or at a playground each discussing our experiences of what had worked and what hadn't. It soon became clear that we were all looking for resources that were not readily available anywhere. We were piecing together what we could from whatever sources we could scavenge. Parents who were interested in beginning to parent bilingually would often confess that they didn't know where to begin. Many had some Spanish in their background but found the prospect of speaking to their kids in Spanish for any length of time a daunting one. How could they go about creating the right environment? Where could they learn the idioms needed for speaking with their kids? These were questions we had to confront in the beginning as well.

We soon developed a network of parents with whom we would share experiences and resources. This motivated us to be more systematic in collecting, recording, and organizing the materials we would ferret out in our own efforts at bilingual parenting. This book grew out of that process and so represents a culmination of our experiences over the past nineteen years in raising our own children. We had to figure out how to obtain materials for our home and how to say the Spanish expressions that come so naturally to us in English. We had to brush up on our Spanish usage and pronunciation. Fortunately, we have had access to native Spanish speakers. They all have been very kind in answering thousands of questions about how to say this or that. Over the years we have compiled these materials and, largely through a process of trial and error but also through some research, we have developed our approach to bilingual parenting. Though the process has sometimes been difficult and frustrating, it has always been fascinating and rewarding. This is why we are now thrilled to be able to pass on this information to you. Read on and let the journey begin.

# THE BILINGUAL HOME

Raising kids bilingually is simply a matter of creating a bilingual environment. There are many ways to do this, and all of them will help you to learn along with your son or daughter. In this chapter we suggest ways to enhance your child's bilingual experience. The more types of Spanish experiences you can bring to your child, the more quickly your child will develop facility in both languages. While all of these ideas may not work for everyone's personal family situation, you can choose the ones that are feasible for you and incorporate as many as you can.

## TALKING

 Talking to kids, in any language, is essential both for language development and for general cognitive development. A recent study indicated that the best predictor of kids' future academic success is whether the family talked during dinner. This factor ranked higher than whether parents read to their children![1] For children learning a second language, talking with their parents is all the more important. When you speak Spanish with them, you will be practicing your own language skills, advancing along with your kids.

---

1. Based on nationally representative surveys of teenagers. National Center on Addiction and Substance Abuse at Columbia University, "The Importance of Family Dinners" (September 2005). http://www.casacolumbia.org/templates/Publications_Reports.aspx#r17.

## Conversational Opportunities

There are many opportunities to converse with kids. Mealtime is one of the best. Another is just before bedtime. At bedtime you can take advantage of your child's natural inclination to stall. One nanosecond before the lights go out, our kids invariably blurt out, "Can I tell you something?" Then they hesitate as they are trying to figure out what to tell us to keep us in the room one more moment. We often just lie down with them and talk for a few moments. Another great opportunity is while reading a book. Here you can ask them questions about what is going to happen, what they think about it, exactly what is happening in the illustration, what else might be going on (where do you think Goldilocks's mother is?), etc. We will help you learn the Spanish you need to do this. Yet another "captive moment" is when your kids are strapped in a car seat.

Conversing with kids means having some questions to ask. After that, you may have trouble getting them to be quiet and eat their dinner. Of course, you have to have the right questions, and this requires a bit of specificity. You'll find help with this too in these pages.

## Who Speaks What?

In a two-parent household, one of the first things that you will have to decide is who is going to speak to whom in which language. One popular method is the "One Parent, One Language" system, which was first formally introduced by French linguist Maurice Grammont in 1902.[2] This is, in fact, the method that Steve and Mary have been applying. Steve speaks Spanish to their kids, and Mary speaks English. The disadvantage of this system for nonnative speakers is that it puts a greater responsibility on the designated Spanish-speaking parent, although it also provides that parent with a greater opportunity to advance in the language.

It is interesting to note how kids progress under the One Parent, One Language approach. If you begin this process at infancy, there are three distinct phases:

---

2. Suzanne Barron-Hauwaert, *Language Strategies for Bilingual Families: The One-Parent-One-Language Approach* (Clevedon, UK: Multilingual Matters, 2004). This book provides a detailed study and interesting discussion of this approach in a variety of situations.

1. *Mixing languages.* As your child first begins to speak, both Spanish and English are used. Spanish words are adopted for some concepts and English words for others. As far as we could tell, our children chose the most easily pronounced word (for example, "book" instead of "libro," "agua" instead of "water").

2. *Assigning languages to persons.* Steve relates: "By about two years old, the kids were speaking strictly English to Mary and strictly Spanish to me. For example, at the dinner table Olivia would tell Mary something in English and then turn to me and, almost in the same breath, switch to Spanish. It was not clear that she even was aware of what language she was speaking or hearing. I experimented by saying something to her in English. Her response was in Spanish. In effect, she had an automatic switch. Each person was assigned a language."

3. *Switching at will.* Somewhere between the ages of five and six, children will discover that they have a choice as to which language to speak. That is, they consciously choose which language they want to speak with whom.

One Parent, One Language is only one of several approaches. Such an approach clearly is not possible for one-parent families. Even two-parent families may find that it does not involve both parents in the experience as much as they would like. Another possibility for two-parent families is to trade off. One day *papi* speaks Spanish, the next *mami* speaks Spanish. A third possibility is to divide the day or the week into Spanish and English. This method is available for both one-parent and two-parent families. (The two-way bilingual public school that our kids attended one year used this system: three days in one language, two in the other.)

Indeed, you may want to switch systems at some point. For example, for Jeff the natural choice in the beginning was to speak English while Emilia, who is Spanish, spoke Spanish to the children. As the kids got older, however, and their English-speaking outside environment (school, etc.) became more influential, they switched to both speaking Spanish in the home as a counterbalance. This is generally referred to as the Minority Language at Home system (MLaH).

There is not much evidence as to which method works best—kids seem to pick up the language irrespective of the method chosen—so you should choose the method that works better for you. The only requirement is that the children have a significant amount of Spanish in their environment and that they hear Spanish at least some of the time from a parent. Speaking Spanish to your kids not only provides them with a vocabulary of words and phrases; it also gives them a powerful role model, especially in the early years. In fact, we believe that the role model function of speaking is more important than the actual content or the grammatical correctness of what you say. Let us once again emphasize the cardinal rule:

> *¡La regla más importante!*
> *(The Most Important Rule!)*
> **Speak to Your Kids in Spanish!**
> (Even if incorrectly.)

When your kids hear you speaking Spanish, they want to do it too. Do not be worried if you are not speaking correctly. Take a cue from your kids. They will freely speak both Spanish and English without the least concern that they are making grammatical errors. So should you. This is great for your progress as well. Language teachers will tell you that one of their greatest challenges is overcoming students' inhibitions, particularly with adults. Instructors strive to create a nonthreatening environment for their students, and most are careful not to "overcorrect" because this stifles language acquisition. If you can get learners to use the target language freely, advancement is nearly assured. Though later on in the process you may have the delightful surprise of occasionally being corrected by your children, they are the perfect guinea pigs for your practice as they are unlikely to be judgmental about your language skills. Particularly in the initial stages, they will pay attention to your content more than to your form. (Minding what you say is another matter!) As you interact with them daily, and for hours each day, you will quickly become accustomed to speaking Spanish at home and will soon find yourself unselfconsciously conversing in Spanish with them in the park or supermarket in front of others. Though Jeff teaches relatively small classes at his university (about twenty students per class) and tries to maximize their speaking opportunities through the use of group and pair work, he estimates that each student's actual speaking time in the classroom is well under two hours a week. When speaking with your kids, your opportunities for meaningful interaction in Spanish will be easily ten or twenty times this amount! It is plain to see how great progress can be made.

In the following sections we will show you how to make sure that your kids get their Spanish from many sources. So you can relax; you will not be their only linguistic model. They will figure out what is right and what is wrong and will soon be correcting you! The most important thing that you can give them is the love of learning, speaking, and understanding Spanish.

## READING

One of the easiest and most rewarding experiences that you can have with your child is reading. ¡Colorín Colorado!, a bilingual website specializing in helping children read, says: "It's never too early to read to your baby. As soon as your baby is born, he or she starts learning. Just by talking to, playing with, and caring for your baby every day, you help your baby develop language skills necessary to become a reader. By reading with your baby, you foster a love of books and reading right from the start."[3]

 In the United States children's books in Spanish are widely available. Many of the most popular English-language children's books have been translated into Spanish, including *Goodnight Moon*, the *Spot* series, *Where the Wild Things Are*, *Going on a Bear Hunt*, and the *Berenstain Bears* series. For older kids there are excellent translations of *Charlotte's Web*, the *Ramona* series, and the wildly popular *Harry Potter* books. In addition, there are many, many children's books by Spanish and Latin American authors. (We have provided a list of sources in the appendix.) These have the important advantage of imparting cultural information as well.

Steve describes his experience this way:

> I have always liked reading to my kids. First, it teaches them a love of reading that they will carry with them all of their lives. Second, when I read to them in Spanish, I am confident that they are getting the correct vocabulary and sentence structure. When I speak off the top of my head, I am more prone to making mistakes. Third, I learn a lot of Spanish myself, new vocabulary and phrases that really help me advance! And, lastly, it is a great way for me to practice pronunciation. I can concentrate on the sound without worrying about grammar and vocabulary.

If you use the One Parent, One Language method, one parent will read in English and the other in Spanish. Again, other approaches are possible, and we vary our routine on occasion. The important thing is to read as much and as often as possible. Your kids will love it!

---

3. From its guide "Tips for Parents of Babies." The website provides free reading tips for children of many ages, downloadable at http://www.colorincolorado.org/guides /readingtips.

## AUDIOBOOKS (ON TAPE, CD, OR MP3)

Children's stories in audio format are readily available in Spanish (see the appendix). Of course, kids always prefer that Mommy or Daddy read to them. Nevertheless, such books do have their advantages. We tend to use them on long car trips, and sometimes we let the kids listen to a book on tape as they are falling asleep at night. Many audiobooks come with a printed book with pictures so that you can read them to your kids as well. One advantage of audiobooks is that you can be assured that the pronunciation is correct. In fact, listening to these books along with your kids is a good way to improve your own comprehension and pronunciation.

## MUSIC

Children tend to love music, and there is a lot of Spanish-language music out there for kids. We listen to music all the time. The kids usually figure out the songs and begin to sing along before we do. They often go to sleep with some kind  of music. In addition to helping with language acquisition, this exposes the kids to music, another discipline that, according to recent studies, is important for cognitive development.[4]

## TELEVISION

When Mary was first pregnant with Olivia, Steve and Mary would discuss the role of television in their soon-to-be-expanded family. Here is how Steve recalls it:

> I argued that we should throw the TV set out the window and live a TV-free existence. (I admit I go to extremes.) I conceded that occasionally there is something valuable on. However, I felt that television just wasn't controllable and that it would end up taking over our lives. Mary was more moderate and argued that we could indeed control what the kids watch and that TV

---

4. Lois Hetland, "Listening to Music Enhances Spatial-Temporal Reasoning: Evidence for the "'Mozart Effect,'" *Journal of Aesthetic Education* 34, no. 3/4, Special Issue: The Arts and Academic Achievement: What the Evidence Shows (Autumn–Winter 2000): 105–148.

certainly would not turn into an electronic babysitter. Our decision to raise our kids bilingually gave us a middle ground in this tug of war. What we finally agreed upon was that we would keep the television but we would limit what the kids watched to programs and movies in Spanish.

Television can be a tremendous asset in language acquisition. Many an immigrant will tell you that he or she learned English primarily by watching American television. Of course, with kids, this can be overdone; limiting our children's TV viewing to programs in Spanish allows us to be sure they are getting something valuable out of it.

What do they watch? Well, we must confess that we have most of the Disney animated children films in Spanish, including *Snow White, Sleeping Beauty, The Great Mouse Detective, The Little Mermaid, Beauty and the Beast,*  *The Lion King,* and many more. There are also many nonanimated kid movies with Spanish soundtracks, including *Mary Poppins, Babe, Free Willy,* and *Fly Away Home,* to name just a few. It is also possible to get a Mexican version of *Sesame Street* (known as *Plaza Sésamo*). (This is not a dubbing of the American version, but rather reflects its Latin American setting. There was also a version, known as *Barrio Sésamo,* that ran for many years in Spain.) Additionally, there are many programs specifically designed for kids who are learning Spanish.

## COMPUTER PROGRAMS

If your kids play on the computer at home, know that there are now many programs specifically designed for kids who are learning Spanish. One that our kids enjoyed was the *Living Books* series, in which a book is read in either English or Spanish and then the kids can play with the interactive images. More programs are becoming available every day, including such favorites as the game *Where in the World Is Carmen Sandiego?*

## CHILD CARE

Many parents require at least some child care during the workday. This represents a tremendous opportunity to give your child or children a bilingual environment. In many communities, child care workers who speak fluent Spanish are readily available. Here are some possible scenarios.

Families often hire child care professionals to come to their houses several times a week to care for their children while the parents are at work. If you can find a child care professional who is also fluent in Spanish, it is important to instruct this person to speak to your children exclusively in Spanish. (Most such professionals also speak fluent English.)

Some parents hire live-in *caregivers* through services that place *au pairs* from foreign countries; others hire live-ins locally. In areas with sizable Hispanic populations, it is often possible to find live-ins who are native Spanish speakers. Universities also are good sources of Spanish-speaking child care. Some university students are willing to exchange child care for rent or for room and board.

Steve and Mary often have exchanged room and board for part-time child care, typically with a young Mexican woman who is hoping to perfect her English. Not only has this been a great source of fluent Spanish for the kids, but it also has been rewarding in many other ways. They have come to know several families in Mexico and have continued to interact with them for years after. Jeff's family has employed several au pairs from Spain who have come to do graduate work at the local university.

In short, if you require some hours of child care each week, it is often possible to make that experience part of your bilingual environment.


## SCHOOL AND PRESCHOOL

Besides individual child care, an increasing number of day care centers, preschools, and schools provide bilingual environments. Over the years, Olivia and Claire (Steve and Mary's daughters) have attended a preschool in which only Spanish was spoken. Their youngest daughter, Saraí, attends a school where Spanish is incorporated into the curriculum. The preschool was little more than a group of parents who got together and hired a bilingual teacher. A local church provided the space.

Bilingual elementary, middle, and high schools are becoming more popular. Other schools and preschools incorporate Spanish into their curricula. Thus opportunities may exist in your community. At least one school that our children attended incorporated Spanish into its curriculum after parents indicated that this would be attractive to them.

**FRIENDS**

This was a greater challenge than we had anticipated. Ideally, we would have found Spanish-speaking friends whom our kids could have gotten to know and play with. However, political rhetoric to the contrary, most kids in this country who speak Spanish fluently also speak English fluently. Although these kids may speak Spanish in their homes, if they sense that your child is more comfortable with English, they will switch to English in a heartbeat.

In spite of the challenges, it pays to be vigilant to whatever opportunities do arise. We occasionally meet families who are new to the country or who are here for short stays and whose kids are native Spanish speakers. Although these opportunities may appear infrequently, they should be seized upon. Not only will they provide Spanish at a peer level for your children, but they also may provide you with contacts and relationships that you may find rewarding later. In its "10 Steps to Raising Multilingual Children," the Multilingual Children's Association calls this "establishing a support network":

> Get your support from others like you. Most things are more fun and rewarding if you share them with like-minded people. Not only do you have a peer group to discuss the art of raising multilingual children and benefit from the experiences of others, but you will build a network of other speakers of your minority language. Equally important, it gives your child the opportunity to hear, speak, and interact with other children in the minority language. This is an enormous motivator for them (this time, group pressure actually works in your favor!). And playgroups are among the best and easiest ways to do it. They may even remain friends with a few of the kids for a long time. Play friends are probably the best way to ensure continuous language exposure over the years—especially when Mom and Dad lose the coolness factor.[5]

One important resource you have now that we did not have when our children were young is social networking via the Internet. It is much easier now to find people with common interests. Popular networking sites, such as Facebook, are avenues for this, or you might use a site such as Meetup (http://www.meetup.com/topics/) in order to locate a group of parents rais-

---

5. http://www.multilingualchildren.org/getting_started/tensteps.html

ing their kids bilingually, or form your own. The founder of one such group in Bloomfield, New Jersey, confesses that she began the group "out of frustration for the lack of support I find in this particular area for bilingual children." Her group has had twenty-four meet-ups so far and now boasts a "membership" of forty-two parents.

If you have room in your house and if you are amenable to such experiences, hosting exchange students, usually high school age, is an excellent way to introduce your children to Spanish-speaking friends. And finally, another great way to find friends and playmates with whom to practice the language is by traveling to Spanish-speaking countries.

## TRAVEL

Travel to Spanish-speaking countries is an excellent way to reinforce the bilingual environment. The advantage of travel is that it surrounds kids with Spanish and helps them realize that Spanish is an everyday part of life in many parts of the world. (It is not just a weird thing that their parents are trying to foist on them.) In addition, the adventure of deciphering this foreign experience creates an excitement and a feeling of accomplishment. Again, kids begin to understand that bilingualism really is something special.

Because of our focus on bilingualism and biculturalism, the nature of our travels has changed somewhat from those we enjoyed in our former, pre-kid days. No more do we embark on trips that promise thirteen cities in fifteen days. Rather, we find a location, typically a small town, and settle in. We get to know the people. Although we do get to make a few side trips to nearby areas of interest, mostly we focus on the people. We take walks; we become frequent visitors at the local park, city pool, or plaza where the kids hang out; and we get to know the neighbors, the local grocer, and the shop owners. Sometimes we have managed to get the kids involved in school.

Travel serves as good Spanish language practice for you and your kids. More importantly, however, it serves as inspiration. It adds excitement to language, especially for older kids. We have spoken to many American kids in our travels who are excited to be able to speak another language, even if just a little bit. Travel also serves to expose kids to another culture, another world. These experiences are immensely enriching, even apart from the linguistic benefits; speaking the language makes them all the more valuable.

## WHICH OPTIONS WORK FOR YOU?

Again, there is no one way to create a bilingual environment for your children. Not all of the ideas we have presented are possible for every family.  It is important, however, that children get frequent exposure to Spanish. And it is important that you, as a parent, are involved, that you, too, find language an important part of your life. Kids really do not need a structured language program. Instead, give them a bilingual environment: books, movies, music, child care, travel. Read to them, talk to them. Learn with them. As gifted language learners, they will do the rest.

# A FEW THINGS ABOUT SPANISH

## WHOSE SPANISH?

Spanish is spoken all over the world. As with any world language, there are many regional variations that are reflected in pronunciation, vocabulary, and grammar. This is true of English as well. The English you hear in England is not the same as that which you hear in the United States, or in Canada, Australia, or India. Even within a single country there are regional variations. For the most part, the differences are minor and colorful and rarely hinder communication. A British citizen is perfectly (or almost perfectly) understood in the United States and vice versa. Nevertheless, when people from non-English-speaking countries undertake to learn English, they must decide which English to learn.

In Spanish we face a similar dilemma. The variations found in Spain are slightly different from those heard in Latin America. Within Latin America there are many regional differences. The Spanish of Mexico differs from that of Cuba. Argentine Spanish and the Spanish of Central America have additional variations, and there are a variety of dialectical differences within each country. In Spain, for example, the Spanish spoken around Madrid is a bit different from that spoken around Seville or Pamplona. Of course, a Spaniard is understood anywhere in Spanish-speaking Latin America, and a Latin American has no problem at all in Spain. Still, given the differences, which dialect do we learn initially?

In spite of the differences, most words in Spanish are universally understood throughout the Spanish-speaking world. Sometimes there will be two words that mean the same thing, one universally understood and one a local expression. In such cases, we will use the universally understood word. Sometimes, however, a choice must be made. Something may be represented by different words in different countries and there may be no common word for it. Also, grammar varies slightly from country to country. Sometimes the choice is between Old World (Spain) usage and New World (Latin America) usage. In such cases, we have chosen to use the pronunciation and conventions of Latin America. We have made this choice for two reasons. First, far more people speak Latin American Spanish than speak the Spanish of Spain. Second, there are more resources available using Latin American Spanish, including books, music, and DVDs.

As we have pointed out, Latin American Spanish has its own regional variations. For example, there is an additional pronoun, *vos*, with its own accompanying verb form, that is used principally in Argentina and Costa Rica (and in some other places as well) and does not exist either in Spain or in most of the rest of Latin America. In this book we will use the most widely accepted grammar and vocabulary.

## WAYS IN WHICH SPANISH DIFFERS FROM ENGLISH

Since you plan to share this journey to bilingualism with your children, you will probably want to study a little bit of Spanish yourself, whether you are starting from scratch or brushing up on your previous knowledge. You have to make up for your lack of language intuition (which you lost along with your youth) with a little studying. Remember that this book is not intended to replace a more complete, systematic study of Spanish for adults. You might want to take some adult education courses if you can fit them into your schedule, or pull out your old language texts for review. Or you can take advantage of the myriad computer programs now available. And it's always a good idea to supplement any visual materials with CDs you can listen to in the car or audio files you can put on your MP3 player. This text will help you along by reinforcing your knowledge, by showing you how to establish an ideal environment for daily, meaningful, and engaging practice—your interaction with your kids—and by supplying you with the words and phrases that make communication with your son or daughter possible, something no other Spanish instruction materials currently available in any medium do.

At the outset, you may find it useful to review some of the ways in which Spanish differs from English. We have provided both a short course in pronunciation and a short set of grammar lessons at the end of this book. If your language skills are rusty, or if you are new to Spanish grammar or pronunciation, you may wish to look at these sections from time to time. Spanish does differ from English in a number of ways. Here are some of the biggest differences, addressed in more detail in the back of the book:

1. Spanish nouns are either masculine or feminine.
2. Adjectives vary according to number and gender.
3. Subject pronouns are usually dropped.
4. There are formal and informal ways of saying *you* in Spanish. Since this book is about talking to children, we almost always use the informal *you*.
5. *Ser* and *estar* are both translated as *to be*. Several other Spanish verbs can also be translated as *to be* in certain contexts.
6. A "personal *a*" is used to distinguish people as grammatical objects.
7. Double negatives—No tengo nada (I don't have nothing)—are OK in Spanish. Indeed, they are often required.

Try to be aware of (but not overwhelmed by) these differences. The upshot of the first three points is that you will talk to a girl slightly differently than to a boy and that you will address several children differently than just one child. For example:

| | |
|---|---|
| John, are you ready? | *Juan, ¿estás listo?* |
| Saraí, are you ready? | *Saraí, ¿estás lista?* |
| John and Peter, are you ready? | *Juan y Pedro, ¿están listos?* |
| Olivia and Claire, are you ready? | *Olivia y Clara, ¿están listas?* |
| Olivia and Pedro, are you ready? | *Olivia y Pedro, ¿están listos?* |

Notice that the adjective *listo* changes according to number and gender. Also, the verb changes according to number. The phrases use the verb *estar*, which means *to be*, rather than *ser*, which also means *to be*. Finally, note that the subject pronoun (*you*, in the English) is dropped in the Spanish.

### PRESENTING DIFFERENCE IN NUMBER AND GENDER

Since number and gender are so important in Spanish, we will always try to indicate the possible variations for the phrases presented in this book. We use a number of devices to accomplish this:

USE OF NAMES: Most often, we will use names to indicate whether the phrase is appropriate to the circumstances.

| | |
|---|---|
| John, do you want to watch a movie? | *Juan, ¿quieres ver una película?* |
| Girls, do you want to watch a movie? | *Niñas, ¿quieren ver una película?* |

PARENTHETICAL (ALL/YOU ALL): Often we will use a parenthetical "all" or "you all" to give singular and plural variations. For example,

| | |
|---|---|
| Do you (all) want to watch a movie? | *¿Quieres (Quieren) ver una película?* |

Thus you would say, "¿Quieres ver una película?" to one child and "¿Quieren ver una película?" to more than one child.
  Or:

| | |
|---|---|
| Don't you (all) throw sand. | *No tires (tiren) arena.* |

This convention is particularly useful for commands, since English drops the subject pronoun (you) in the command form. This simply means that if you were talking to one child you would say "No tires arena," and if you were talking to more than one child you would say "No tiren arena."

### THE BOTTOM LINE

Always keep in mind that there are many ways to say almost anything. Ultimately, you will learn the expressions that apply to your own personal situation. If you have one daughter, you will learn to use the feminine singular forms of adjectives more often. If you have two boys, you will learn to think in not only masculine and plural terms but also masculine and singular for those one-on-ones. Finally, as you read the different variations of the phrases that we have presented, you will begin to internalize intuitively some of the grammar. In that sense, you will be learning with your kids.

# A
# PHRASE BOOK
## FOR
# TALKING TO KIDS

# HOW TO USE THIS PHRASE BOOK

We designed this book to be used as a reference. It contains a detailed table of contents and index/glossary. Suppose that you want to tell your child to wash her hands but you cannot recall the correct way to say it. You can go to the table of contents and find the chapter "In the Bathroom." A quick search of this chapter (all chapters are short) reveals the phrase that you want. Alternatively, you could look up *wash* in the index. This also will direct you to the desired phrase.

This book is designed for quick utilization. We have avoided lengthy discussions on all the possible ways to render a phrase. Later on, you may find it fascinating to learn that there is a cute phrase for a particular expression in the Dominican Republic or that Argentines say it a bit differently. For now, you just need something quick and correct.

Of course, you will not be able to grab this book every time you need to say something to your child. (Imagine that Susie is beating up Johnnie and you are searching for the phrase that communicates, "Leave your little brother alone!") One possible approach is, after the fact, to look up the phrase that you had needed for the next opportunity. You may not have to wait long. Another possible approach that is quite effective is to pick a phrase that you think is likely to be used during the day and to learn it before going to bed the night before or just as you get up in the morning. Then look for opportunities to use it. You will be surprised how fast this phrase-a-day method works. Keep in mind that if you use a phrase once with a child, you are going to use it again and again and again. That is the nature of talking to children. You say things over and over. While this sometimes can be tedious and even exasperating in your native tongue, when learning a foreign language it is just what the doctor ordered.

# GETTING UP, GETTING GOING

## GOOD MORNING!

**KEY VOCABULARY:**

bed, *la cama*
grumpy, *gruñón/gruñona*
in a good (bad) mood, *de buen (mal) humor*
it's time to, *es hora de*
morning, *la mañana*

to get ready, *prepararse*
to get up, *levantarse*
to sleep, *dormir*
to stretch, *estirarse*
to wake up, *despertarse*

---

### Buenos días

The most common morning greeting is just

Good morning                     *Buenos días.*

You can use this greeting anytime before one o'clock in the afternoon. While we are at it, we might as well learn the following:

Good afternoon                   *Buenas tardes.*
Good evening                     *Buenas noches.*

You can see from above that *el día* is masculine while *la tarde* and *la noche* are feminine. Although most nouns that end in –*a* are feminine, some are not.

## How did you sleep?

The most common way of asking people if they had a good night's sleep is the following:

| | |
|---|---|
| How did you (all) sleep? | *¿Cómo amaneciste (amanecieron)?* |

Literally translated, this means "How did you dawn?" But it really means "Did you have a good night?" or "How did you sleep?" or "How are you this morning?" Typical answers are:

| | |
|---|---|
| Well. | *Bien.* |
| Poorly. | *Mal.* |

A more literal, less common, yet perfectly fine way of asking how people slept is to ask them just that.

| | |
|---|---|
| Olivia, how did you sleep? | *Olivia, ¿cómo dormiste?* |
| Girls, how did you all sleep? | *Niñas, ¿cómo durmieron?* |

The above constructions, *amaneciste, amanecieron, dormiste, durmieron,* are all in the past and thus use the simple past tense of the verbs. You will eventually start to recognize the differences among tenses (present, simple past, imperfect, future), but for now, you should just memorize the phrases. You will use these over and over again and thus learn the way your kids learn. Again, you are learning a vocabulary of phrases. (If you are eager to understand the grammar be-hind these phrases, please see our grammar section, "Grammar Enough to Get You Started.")

## How are you?

Let us continue . . .

| | |
|---|---|
| How are you (all) this morning? | *¿Cómo estás (están) esta mañana?* |
| Great! | *¡Estupendamente!* |
| Marvelous! | *¡De maravilla!* |
| George, you are in a bad mood today. | *Jorge, estás de mal humor hoy.* |
| Alicia, you are happy today. | *Alicia, estás contenta hoy.* |

We will soon discover that there are several ways to render *to be* in Spanish. The verb *estar*, used in the above phrases, is used to convey states (temporary conditions) and locations. Sometimes, however, other verbs will be used to convey one's condition. In the morning, you might ask:

| | |
|---|---|
| Are you (all) sleepy this morning? | *¿Tienes (Tienen) sueño esta mañana?* |
| Are you (all) hungry this morning? | *¿Tienes (Tienen) hambre esta mañana?* |
| Are you (all) thirsty? | *¿Tienes (Tienen) sed?* |
| Yes, I am very hungry. | *Sí, tengo mucha hambre.* |

That is, rather than being hungry, one "has (a lot of) hunger." This also applies to thirst, sleepiness, and a variety of other attributes. (See our grammar section, "Grammar Enough to Get You Started," for more.)

---

**VOCABULARY NOTE**

*Mañana* means both *morning* and *tomorrow*. You can tell which by the context. For example: *Nos vemos mañana por la mañana.* (We'll see each other tomorrow in the morning.)

---

### It seems that . . .

Sometimes you may have your own observations. These can be expressed using the phrase *Parece que* (It seems that) and then adding your observations. *Parece que* is a tremendously useful phrase in all sorts of contexts.

| | |
|---|---|
| It seems like you (all) have a lot of energy today. | *Parece que tienes (tienen) mucha energía hoy.* |
| Margaret, it seems that you're sad today. | *Margarita, parece que estás triste hoy.* |

### You seem . . .

With adjectives, you can shorten the above construction a bit.

| | |
|---|---|
| Saraí, you seem grumpy today. | *Saraí, pareces gruñona hoy.* |
| Boys, you seem happy this morning. | *Niños, parecen contentos esta mañana.* |

## Time to get up

Sometimes waking up and getting going may require a little encouragement.

| | |
|---|---|
| Dear, it is time to wake up. | *Cariño, es hora de despertarte.* |
| Kids, it is time to wake up. | *Niños, es hora de despertarse.* |
| Son, it's time to get up. | *Hijo, es hora de levantarte.* |
| Girls, it is time for you all to get up. | *Niñas, es hora de levantarse.* |
| Claire, it's time to get ready for school. | *Clara, es hora de prepararte para la escuela.* |
| Boys, it is time to get ready for school. | *Niños, es hora de prepararse para la escuela.* |

Notice the *te* and *se* in the above phrases. *Despertar* is to wake (someone else) up. *Despertarse* is to wake oneself up. When someone does something to oneself, we call it (grammatically) a reflexive or pronominal construction. Spanish often requires a reflexive construction when English may not. Consider:

| | |
|---|---|
| Wake up your brother, please. | *Despierta a tu hermano, por favor.* |
| Wake up, please. | *Despiértate, por favor.* |
| Let's stretch! | *¡Vamos a estirarnos!* |

For more on these types of verbs, see the lesson on Pronominal Verbs in our grammar section, "Grammar Enough to Get You Started."

## The Morning Song

This song is sung to the tune of "Frère Jacques" (Are you sleeping?):

| | |
|---|---|
| Good morning. | *Buenos días.* |
| Good morning. 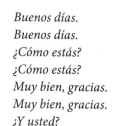 | *Buenos días.* |
| How are you? | *¿Cómo estás?* |
| How are you? | *¿Cómo estás?* |
| Very well, thank you. | *Muy bien, gracias.* |
| Very well, thank you. | *Muy bien, gracias.* |
| How about you? | *¿Y usted?* |
| How about you?  | *¿Y usted?* |

# THE WEATHER

**KEY VOCABULARY:**

cloud, *la nube*
cold, *el frío*
fall, *el otoño*
fog, *la niebla*
heat, *el calor*
moon, *la luna*
rain, *la lluvia*
snow, *la nieve*
spring, *la primavera*
star, *la estrella*

storm, la *tormenta*
summer, *el verano*
sun, *el sol*
weather, *el tiempo*
winter, *el invierno*

to drizzle, *lloviznar, chispear*
to hail, *granizar*
to rain, *llover*
to snow, *nevar*

---

**VOCABULARY NOTE**

*Tiempo* means both *time* and *weather*. You can tell which by the context.

---

> ### How's the weather?

For some expressions, Spanish uses *hacer* (to make, do) where English uses *to be*.

What is the weather like today?    *¿Qué tiempo hace hoy?*
It is (very) hot.    *Hace (mucho) calor.*
It is (very) cold.    *Hace (mucho) frío.*
It is cool.    *Hace fresco.*
It is (very) nice out today.    *Hace (muy) buen tiempo hoy.*
It is (very) windy.    *Hace (mucho) aire.*

If there is some kind of precipitation outside, then we express it much as we would in English. *Está* means *it is*, and then we use the present participle of the verb. (See "Grammar Enough to Get You Started" to learn how to form present participles.)

It is raining.    *Está lloviendo.*
It is pouring.    *Está lloviendo a chorros (a cántaros).*

| It is drizzling. | *Está lloviznando.* |
| It is snowing. | *Está nevando.* |
| It is hailing. | *Está granizando.* |

The word *hay* means *there is* or *there are*. You can use this construction to explain what is outside (snow, ice, sun, clouds, etc.):

| There is snow on the ground. | *Hay nieve en el suelo.* |
| It is icy outside. | *Hay hielo afuera.* |
| It is sunny. | *Hay sol.* |
| There is a lot of mud outside. | *Hay mucho lodo afuera.* |
| There are lots of clouds today. | *Hay muchas nubes hoy.* |
| There is fog. | *Hay niebla.* |

You can use *está* with an adjective to point to conditions.

| It is slippery outside. | *Está resbaloso afuera.* |
| It is wet outside. | *Todo está mojado afuera.* |
| It is very muddy outside. | *Está muy lodoso afuera.* |
| It is sunny. | *Está soleado.* |
| It is cloudy. | *Está nublado.* |

Here are some additional useful expressions:

| It seems like it is going to rain. | *Parece que va a llover.* |
| They say a storm is coming. | *Dicen que viene una tormenta.* |
| Claire, look at the lightning. | *Clara, mira los relámpagos (rayos).* |
| Adrian and Alexandra, look at the rain. | *Adrián y Alejandra, miren la lluvia.* |
| Jude, listen to the thunder. | *Judas, escucha los truenos.* |
| Olivia and David, listen to the hail. | *Olivia y David, escuchen el granizo.* |
| Another rainy day! | *¡Otro día de lluvia!* |
| | *¡Otro día lluvioso!* |

## What do you think?

Everyone has an opinion about the weather. You may want to ask your kids:

| What is the weather like today? | *¿Qué tiempo hace hoy?* |
| | *¿Cómo está el día hoy?* |

| | |
|---|---|
| Robert and David, what do you think? | *Roberto y David, ¿qué les parece?* |
| Is it going to snow? | *¿Va a nevar?* |
| Laura, do you think that it is going to rain? | *Laura, ¿crees que va a llover?* |
| Saraí and Sam, do you think that it is cold outside? | *Saraí y Sam, ¿creen que hace frío afuera?* |
| Claire, are you hot? | *Clara, ¿tienes calor?* |
| Boys, are you cold? | *Niños, ¿tienen frío?* |

## The seasons (Las estaciones)

| | |
|---|---|
| In the winter, it is cold and there is a lot of snow. | *En el invierno, hace frío y hay mucha nieve.* |
| In the spring, there are lots of flowers. | *En la primavera, hay muchas flores.* |
| In the summer, we can go to the beach. | *En el verano, podemos ir a la playa.* |
| In the fall, the leaves change color. | *En el otoño, las hojas cambian de color.* |

**GETTING DRESSED**

**KEY VOCABULARY (CLOTHES):**

clothes/clothing, *la ropa* (note that it is singular in Spanish)
backpack, *la mochila*
blouse, *la blusa*
glasses, *los lentes, las gafas*
jacket, *la chaqueta*
pants, *los pantalones*
raincoat, *el impermeable*
shirt, *la camisa*
shoes, *los zapatos*

shorts, *un short, un pantalón corto*
socks, *los calcetines*
sunglasses, *gafas de sol*
sweater, *el suéter*
tie (necktie), *la corbata*
tights, *las medias*
umbrella, *el paraguas*
undershirt, *la camiseta*
underwear, *la ropa interior*
underpants (boys' and girls'), *los calzones*

| Time to get dressed |
| --- |

|  |  |
| --- | --- |
| John, it is time to get dressed. | *Juan, es hora de vestirte.* |
| Teresa and Amanda, it is time to dress. | *Teresa y Amanda, es hora de vestirse.* |
| John, it is time to put on your clothes for school. | *Juan, es hora de ponerte la ropa para la escuela.* |
| Teresa and Amanda, it is time to put on your clothes for school. | *Teresa y Amanda, es hora de ponerse la ropa para la escuela.* |

After school you may find yourself saying this.

|  |  |
| --- | --- |
| James, will you change your clothes, please? | *Jaime, ¿quieres cambiarte la ropa, por favor?* |
| Girls, will you change your clothes? | *Niñas, ¿quieren cambiarse la ropa?* |

---

**GRAMMAR NOTE**

Spanish often uses a reflexive construction to denote possession. Instead of saying, "Put on *your* clothes," a literal (albeit awkward) translation of the Spanish might be "Put the clothes on *yourself.*" For more on this, please see our grammar section, "Grammar Enough to Get You Started."

## Oh, what to wear?

| | |
|---|---|
| John, what do you want to wear today? | *Juan, ¿qué quieres ponerte hoy?* |
| Isabel and Mary, what do you want to wear today? | *Isabel y María, ¿qué quieren ponerse hoy?* |
| John, do you want to wear pants or shorts? | *Juan, ¿quieres ponerte pantalones o un short?* |

---

**VOCABULARY NOTE**

*Un short* is one of those English imports common in Spanish. You could also use *un pantalón corto*, but it is less common.

---

| | |
|---|---|
| Ellen, do you want to wear a dress today? | *Elena, ¿quieres ponerte un vestido hoy?* |
| Adrian, put on your socks. | *Adrián, ponte los calcetines.* |
| Isabel and Mary, put on your shoes. | *Isabel y María, pónganse los zapatos.* |
| John, will you put on your shirt? | *Juan, ¿quieres ponerte la camisa?* |
| John, will you tuck in your shirt? | *Juan, ¿quieres meter la camisa?* |
| Mary and Ellen, can you put on your skirts? | *María y Elena, ¿quieren ponerse la falda?* |
| Mary and Ellen, will you tuck in your blouses? | *María y Elena, ¿quieren meter la blusa?* |

---

**GRAMMAR NOTE**

Note that, unlike in English, *falda* (skirt) is singular in the above construction. Another example: *Los hombres se pusieron el sombrero y se fueron.* (The men put on their hats and left.)

---

| | |
|---|---|
| Tony, did you put on clean underwear? | *Antonio, ¿te pusiste ropa interior limpia?* |
| Irene and Sophia, did you put on clean underwear? | *Irene y Sofía, ¿se pusieron ropa interior limpia?* |
| Irene, go and get a clean undershirt. | *Irene, ve a buscar una camiseta limpia.* |

| | |
|---|---|
| Isabel and Mary, go and get a clean pair of panties. | *Isabel y María, vayan a buscar unos calzones[1] limpios.* |

---

**VOCABULARY NOTE**

Although *buscar* literally means *to look for*, it is also used to mean *to go and get*.

---

| | |
|---|---|
| Mario, your belt is in your drawer. | *Mario, tu cinturón está en tu cajón.* |
| Matt, your shirts are on the bottom shelf. | *Mateo, tus camisas están en el estante de abajo.* |
| Girls, your panties are in the top drawer. | *Niñas, sus calzones están en el cajón de arriba.* |
| Girls, your scarves are in the middle closet. | *Niñas, sus bufandas están en el armario de en medio.* |
| Daniel, you have to wear playclothes today. | *Daniel, tienes que llevar ropa de jugar hoy.* |
| Ana and Claire, you have to wear clothes for the park today. | *Ana y Clara, tienen que llevar ropa para el parque hoy.* |
| Jude, you need warm clothes today. | *Judas, necesitas ropa de abrigo hoy.* |
| Roberto and Olivia, you need a raincoat. | *Robert y Olivia, necesitan un impermeable.* |
| Ricky, you cannot wear those shoes. | *Riki, no puedes llevar esos zapatos.* |
| Those shoes are too slippery. | *Esos zapatos son demasiado resbalosos.* |
| Ana and Claire, you cannot wear a fancy dress today. | *Ana y Clara, no pueden llevar un vestido elegante hoy.* |
| Gabriela, will you find me your glasses, please? | *Gabriela, ¿quieres encontrarme tus gafas, por favor?* |

## Zippers, buttons, shoelaces, oh my

| | |
|---|---|
| Angela, button your blouse please. | *Ángela, abróchate la blusa, por favor.* |
| Angela, can you button your blouse? | *Ángela, ¿puedes abrocharte la blusa?* |
| George and Peter, button your shirts. | *Jorge y Pedro, abróchense la camisa.* |

---

1. *Los calzones* refers to both girls' panties and boys' underpants. Kids often shorten this to *los chones*.

| | |
|---|---|
| George and Peter, can you button your shirts? | *Jorge y Pedro, ¿pueden abrocharse la camisa?* |
| George, can you zip up your zipper? | *Jorge, ¿puedes subir la cremallera?* |
| Martha, tie your shoes. | *Marta, amárrate los zapatos.* |
| Martha, will you tie your shoelaces? | *Marta, ¿quieres amarrarte los zapatos?* |
| Saraí and James, tie your shoes. | *Saraí y Jaime, amárrense los zapatos.* |
| Patricia and James, can you tie your shoes? | *Patricia y Jaime, ¿pueden amarrarse los zapatos?* |

## Backward, inside out, upside down

In Spanish, *backward*, *inside out*, and *reversed* are all expressed by *al revés*.

| | |
|---|---|
| Julie, your dress is on backwards. | *Julia, tu vestido está al revés.* |
| Michael, your shirt is on inside out. | *Miguel, tu camisa está al revés.* |
| Paul, your shoes are on the wrong feet. | *Pablo, tus zapatos están al revés.* |

If you want to distinguish between inside out and backward, you could say:

| | |
|---|---|
| Julie, your dress is on backward. | *Julia, traes lo de delante para atrás.* |

Sometimes you may just want to point out that your kid has done something funny and then let him or her figure it out.

| | |
|---|---|
| Samuel, you made a mistake with your shirt. | *Samuel, te equivocaste con la camisa.* |

## A helping hand

| | |
|---|---|
| Olivia, do you need help? | *Olivia, ¿necesitas ayuda?* |
| Do you know how to tie your shoes? | *¿Sabes amarrarte los zapatos?* |
| May I help you to tie your shoes? | *¿Puedo ayudarte a amarrarte los zapatos?* |

| | |
|---|---|
| May I tie your shoes? | *¿Puedo amarrarte los zapatos?* |
| Daniel and Michael, do you need help? | *Daniel y Miguel, ¿necesitan ayuda?* |
| Do you know how to button your shirts? | *¿Saben abrocharse la camisa?* |
| May I help you to button your shirts? | *¿Puedo ayudarlos a abrocharse la camisa?* |
| Daniel and Michael, may I button your shirts? | *Daniel y Miguel, ¿puedo abrocharles la camisa?* |
| Ellen, can you do it by yourself? | *Elena, ¿puedes hacerlo sola?* |
| Ellen and David, can you do it by yourselves? | *Elena y David, ¿pueden hacerlo solos?* |

---

**GRAMMAR NOTE**

The following phrases use the command form of the verbs (*dejar* and *tratar*). For more on how to form commands in Spanish (and how to avoid them altogether), see our grammar section, "Grammar Enough to Get You Started."

---

| | |
|---|---|
| Olivia, let me tie your shoes. | *Olivia, déjame amarrarte los zapatos.* |
| Daniel and Michael, let me button your shirts. | *Daniel y Miguel, déjenme abrocharles la camisa.* |
| Paul, try to do it yourself. | *Pablo, trata de hacerlo solo.* |
| Girls, try to do it yourselves. | *Niñas, traten de hacerlo solas.* |

And here are a couple of phrases just to memorize. (The specific grammar is beyond the scope of this book.)

| | |
|---|---|
| Adrian, do you want me to do it? | *Adrián, ¿quieres que lo haga yo?* |
| Olivia and Claire, do you want me to do it? | *Olivia y Clara, ¿quieren que lo haga yo?* |

## I like the way you look

| | |
|---|---|
| Marcela, I like your dress. | *Marcela, me gusta tu vestido.* |
| Marcela and Victoria, I like your shoes. | *Marcela y Victoria, me gustan sus zapatos.* |

| | |
|---|---|
| Henry, I like your socks. | *Enrique, me gustan tus calcetines.* |
| What a nice dress. | *Qué vestido más bonito.* |
| What nice shoes. | *Qué zapatos más bonitos.* |

---

**GRAMMAR NOTE**

To say *like*, Spanish uses the verb *gustar*, which means *to be pleasing to*. Thus *Me gustan tus calcetines* literally translates as "Your socks are pleasing to me." The word *calcetines* is the subject, and thus *gustan* is third-person plural.

---

| | |
|---|---|
| Look at yourself in the mirror. | *Mírate en el espejo.* |
| Rose, try not to get messed up. | *Rosa, trata de no desarreglarte.* |
| Boys, try not to get dirty. | *Niños, traten de no ensuciarse.* |
| Richard, try not to mess up your hair. | *Ricardo, trata de no despeinarte.* |

# ACCESSORIES, HAIR, AND MAKEUP

**KEY VOCABULARY:**

bangs, *el flequillo*
barette, *un broche, un pasador*
bracelet, *la pulsera, el brazalete*
braid, *una trenza*
brush, *un cepillo*
comb, *el peine*
earrings, *los aretes, los pendientes*
hair, *el pelo, el cabello*
hairband (head-size, U-shaped plastic band), *una diadema*
hair dryer, *el secador de cabello*
headband (head-size cloth band), *una banda*

lipstick, *el lápiz de labios*
nail polish, *el esmalte de uñas*
necklace, *un collar*
pigtails, tails, *unas colitas*
ponytail, *una colita de caballo*
ponytail holder (small elastic), *una liga*
ponytail holder (large cloth elastic), *una dona*
ring, *un anillo*
watch, *el reloj*
to comb, *peinar*
to brush, *cepillar*

## Accessories are everything

| | |
|---|---|
| Ellen, are you going to wear earrings today? | *Elena, ¿vas a llevar aretes hoy?* |
| Which earrings are you going to wear? | *¿Qué aretes vas a llevar?* |
| Mary, do you want to put on a necklace? | *María, ¿quieres ponerte un collar?* |
| Mary and Claire, do you want to put on necklaces? | *María y Clara, ¿quieren ponerse un collar?* |
| Who wants to put on a bracelet? | *¿Quién quiere ponerse una pulsera?* |
| Carl, don't forget your watch. | *Carlos, no olvides tu reloj.* |
| Julia and Roberta, don't forget your watches. | *Julia y Roberta, no olviden su reloj.* |
| Victoria, where is your ring? | *Victoria, ¿dónde está tu anillo?* |

## Hair issues

| | |
|---|---|
| Edward, it is time to comb your hair. | *Eduardo, es hora de peinarte.* |
| Paula, it is time to brush your hair. | *Paula, es hora de cepillarte el pelo.* |

| | |
|---|---|
| Henry, will you comb your hair, please? | Enrique, ¿quieres peinarte, por favor? |
| Paula, can you brush your hair, please? | Paula, ¿puedes cepillarte el pelo, por favor? |
| Robert, let me comb your hair. | Roberto, déjame peinarte. |
| Girls, let me brush your hair. | Niñas, déjenme cepillarles el pelo. |
| Jane, you need to dry your hair. | Juana, tienes que secarte el pelo. |
| I am going to get the hair dryer. | Voy a buscar el secador de cabello. |
| Catherine, do you want braids? | Catarina, ¿quieres trenzas? |
| Do you want a ponytail? | ¿Quieres una colita de caballo? |
| Mercedes, do you want pigtails? | Mercedes, ¿quieres colitas? |
| Ann, do you want bangs? | Ana, ¿quieres el flequillo? |
| Let me brush your bangs. | Déjame cepillarte el flequillo. |
| Girls, choose some barrettes. | Niñas, escojan unos broches. |
| I'm going to put a barrette here and a ponytail here. | Voy a ponerte un broche aquí y una colita de caballo aquí. |
| Teresa, don't take out the barrettes. | Teresa, no te quites los broches. |
| Julia, go and get a hair band. | Julia, ve a buscar una diadema. |
| Girls, go and get a cloth headband. | Niñas, vayan a buscar una banda. |
| Who wants some gel? | ¿Quién quiere gel? |
| I am going to put some water in your hair. | Voy a ponerte un poco de agua en el pelo. |
| Don't move. | No te muevas. |
| Be still, please. | Estate quieto, por favor. |

## Makeup, anyone?

| | |
|---|---|
| Who wants to put on some makeup? | ¿Quién quiere ponerse maquillaje? |
| Ellen, do you want to paint your fingernails? | Elena, ¿quieres pintarte las uñas? |
| Ellen and Jane, do you want to paint your nails? | Elena y Juana, ¿quieren pintarse las uñas? |
| Jane, can you bring me the nail polish? | Juana, ¿puedes traerme el esmalte de uñas? |
| Ellen, what color do you want? | Elena, ¿qué color quieres? |
| Isabel, do you want to put on lipstick? | Isabel, ¿quieres ponerte lápiz de labios? |

**GRAMMAR NOTE**

There are some quirks in the ways Spanish speakers express color. See "Colors" in our grammar section, "Grammar Enough to Get You Started," for some notes on color as well as a list of the most common ones.

## MOVING ABOUT

**KEY VOCABULARY:**

bathroom, *el cuarto de baño, el baño*
bedroom, *el dormitorio, el cuarto, la recámara (Mex.), la habitación*
dining room, *el comedor*
floor, *el piso*
    second floor, *segundo piso*
    the downstairs, *piso de abajo*
    the upstairs, *piso de arriba*
grass, *la hierba*
kitchen, *la cocina*
laundry room, *la lavandería*
lawn, *el césped*
living room, *la sala*
office, *la oficina*

porch, *el porche*
    front porch, *el porche de delante*
    back porch, *el porche de atrás*
room, *el cuarto*
stairs, *la escalera*
study, *el estudio*
yard, *el jardín*
    front yard, *el jardín de delante*
    back yard, *el jardín de atrás*

to come, *venir*
to go, *ir*
to go (come) up, *subir*
to go (come) down, *bajar*

---

### Coming and going

This short chapter is devoted to navigation, how to get from here to there, and how to change position. Let's start with coming and going.

| | |
|---|---|
| Saraí, come here, please. | *Saraí, ven acá (aquí), por favor.*[2] |
| Boys, come here, please. | *Niños, vengan acá, por favor.* |

Now here is a tricky one for English speakers. Suppose that your child has called you. "*Mami, ven acá.*" What do you say as you are on your way? In English you would call, "I'm coming." In Spanish, the correct expression is *Voy* (I'm going). Thus the sequence you would hear in corresponding English- and Spanish-speaking homes is this:

| | |
|---|---|
| Mom, come here, please. | *Mami, ven acá (aquí), por favor.* |
| I'm coming. | *Voy.* |

---

2. Both *acá* and *aquí* are used to refer to something close to the speaker. Generally, *acá* is less specific, meaning something like "around here." However, in many places in Latin America, it is the most common way to say "here."

If movement is toward the speaker, use *venir*. If movement is away from the speaker, use *ir*. The same rules apply with *llevar* (to take) and *traer* (to bring).

These little differences are the things that make language study so interesting. On the other hand, if you mess up—if you say *¡Vengo!* (I'm coming!) instead of *¡Voy!* (I'm going!)—your kid will survive. Again, it is important to speak Spanish even if you occasionally, or even frequently, mess up.

| | |
|---|---|
| Gabriela, will you take this to Dad? | *Gabriela, ¿quieres llevarle esto a papi?* |
| Boys, will you bring me your shoes? | *Niños, ¿quieren traerme los zapatos?* |
| You (all) need to take a present to the birthday party. | *Tienes (tienen) que llevar algo a la fiesta de cumpleaños.* |

## Upstairs, downstairs

If your house has more than one floor, you will find the following useful.

| | |
|---|---|
| My room is upstairs. | *Mi cuarto está en el piso de arriba (en el piso superior).* |
| The laundry room is downstairs. | *La lavandería está en el piso de abajo (en el piso inferior).* |

If you are downstairs and are referring to upstairs, or if you are upstairs and referring to downstairs, you can simplify the above expressions:

| | |
|---|---|
| My room is upstairs. | *Mi cuarto está arriba.* |
| The laundry room is downstairs. | *La lavandería está abajo.* |

Telling someone to go upstairs or downstairs is accomplished in Spanish with the verbs *subir* (to go up) and *bajar* (to go down).

| | |
|---|---|
| Claudia, go upstairs to your room and look for your shoes. | *Claudia, sube a tu cuarto y busca tus zapatos.* |
| Boys, go upstairs to the bathroom. | *Niños, suban al baño.* |
| Roger, go downstairs to the living room and pick up your toys. | *Rogelio, baja a la sala y recoge tus juguetes.* |
| Girls, go downstairs and get your clothes. | *Niñas, bajen a buscar su ropa.* |

| | |
|---|---|
| Girls, will you go downstairs and get your toys, please? | *Niñas, ¿quieren bajar a buscar sus juguetes, por favor?* |

## Standing up and lying down

In Latin America the standard way to say *stand up* is with the verb *pararse*.

| | |
|---|---|
| Christine, stand up please. | *Cristina, párate, por favor.* |
| Christine is standing. | *Cristina está parada.* |
| Boys, stand up, please. | *Niños, párense, por favor.* |
| The boys are standing. | *Los niños están parados.* |

---

**VOCABULARY NOTE**

In Latin American Spanish, the verb *pararse* means *to stand up*. The verb *parar* (nonreflexive) means *to stop*. Thus we have *¡Para!* (Stop!) or *¡Para de hacer eso!* (Stop doing that!). On the other hand, we have *Párate, por favor.* (Stand up, please.)

---

To lie down is *acostarse*, and to be lying down is *estar acostado*. *Acostarse* is the same verb that you use for going to bed.

| | |
|---|---|
| James, please lie down. | *Jaime, acuéstate, por favor.* |
| James is lying down. | *Jaime está acostado.* |
| Girls, lie down. | *Niñas, acuéstense.* |
| The girls are lying down. | *Las niñas están acostadas.* |

## Sitting down and sitting up

To sit down is *sentarse*, and to be sitting down is *estar sentado*.

| | |
|---|---|
| Margaret, sit down, please. | *Margarita, siéntate, por favor.* |
| Paula and Rose, sit down here. | *Paula y Rosa, siéntense aquí.* |
| Michael, will you sit down? | *Miguel, ¿quieres sentarte?* |
| Boys, will you sit down, please? | *Niños, ¿quieren sentarse, por favor?* |
| Margaret, are you sitting down? | *Margarita, ¿estás sentada?* |
| Boys, are you sitting down? | *Niños, ¿están sentados?* |

To sit up from a lying-down position is *incorporarse*.

| Hugh, sit up, please. | *Hugo, incorpórate, por favor.* |
| Hugh, will you sit up? | *Hugo, ¿quieres incorporarte?* |

If you want to say "sit up straight" (from a slouching position), you need to use another verb:

| Amanda, sit up straight. | *Amanda, siéntate derecha.* |
| Boys, sit up straight. | *Niños, siéntense derechos.* |

## Kneeling and squatting

For kneeling or squatting we have the following constructions:

| Christine, kneel down. | *Cristina, ponte de rodillas.* |
| | *Cristina, arrodíllate.* |
| Christine, are you kneeling? | *Cristina, ¿estás de rodillas?* |
| | *Cristina, ¿estás arrodillada?* |
| Boys, squat down. | *Niños, pónganse de cuclillas.* |
| | *Niños, agáchense.* |
| Boys, are you squatting? | *Niños, ¿están de cuclillas?* |

Finally, our kids are always saying, "*Agáchate, papi*," which simply means, "Stoop down, Daddy."

# IN THE BATHROOM

## GOING TO THE BATHROOM

**KEY VOCABULARY:**

bathroom, *el cuarto de baño, el baño*
peepee, *el pipí*
poopie, *la caca, el popó*
toilet, *el inodoro*
toilet paper, *el papel higiénico*
wet, *mojado*

to clean (wipe), *limpiar*
to have to, *tener que*
to wet, *mojar*
to get wet, *mojarse*

### Getting there, using it

Probably the first thing to learn here is how to get to the bathroom and use it.

| | |
|---|---|
| David, do you have to go to the bathroom? | *David, ¿tienes que ir al baño?* |
| Girls, do you have to go to the bathroom? | *Niñas, ¿tienen que ir al baño?* |

Of course, you can be a lot more specific.

| | |
|---|---|
| David, do you have to go poopie? | *David, ¿tienes que hacer caca (popó)?* |
| Girls, do you have to go peepee? | *Niñas, ¿tienen que hacer pipí?* |

---

**VOCABULARY NOTE**

*Tener que* means *to have to*. It is a tremendously useful phrase. A similar phrase is *Hay que* which means *It is necessary to*. Thus you could say, *Tienes que lavarte las manos* (You have to wash your hands) or *Hay que lavarse las manos* (It is necessary to wash hands). The second expression is more impersonal.

---

Or:

| | |
|---|---|
| Alfred, do you want to go to the bathroom? | *Alfredo, ¿quieres ir al baño?* |
| Girls, do you want to go peepee? | *Niñas, ¿quieren hacer pipí?* |

Or, more insistent:

| | |
|---|---|
| David, will you go peepee? | *David, ¿quieres ir a hacer pipí?* |
| Mark, go peepee, please. | *Marcos, ve a hacer pipí, por favor.* |
| Girls, go peepee. | *Niñas, vayan a hacer pipí.* |

Sometimes you will want to know whether the endeavor was successful.

| | |
|---|---|
| Martin, did you go poopie? | *Martín, ¿hiciste popó?* |
| Girls, did you go peepee? | *Niñas, ¿hicieron pipí?* |

## After poopie

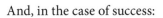

And, in the case of success:

| | |
|---|---|
| Patricia, can you wipe yourself? | *Patricia, ¿puedes limpiarte la colita (el culito)?* |
| Victor, do you need help? | *Víctor, ¿necesitas ayuda?* |
| Eve, are you ready? | *Eva, ¿estás lista?* |
| Ernest, are you ready to wipe yourself? | *Ernesto, ¿estás listo para limpiarte la colita?* |
| Patricia, do you need toilet paper? | *Patricia, ¿necesitas papel higiénico?* |
| Claire, can you flush the toilet? | *Clara, ¿puedes jalar de la cadena?* |

> **VOCABULARY NOTE**
>
> *Jalar de la cadena* literally means "pull the chain" and comes from when most toilets had water tanks mounted high up and were flushed by pulling the chain attached to the tank. Other common ways of saying "flush the toilet" are *bajarle al inodoro* and *bajarle a la taza*.

| | |
|---|---|
| Andrew, wash your hands please. | *Andrés, lávate las manos, por favor.* |
| Girls, wash your hands with soap. | *Niñas, lávense las manos con jabón.* |
| Albert, did you wash your hands with soap? | *Alberto, ¿te lavaste las manos con jabón?* |
| Girls, did you wash your hands? | *Niñas, ¿se lavaron las manos?* |
| Paula, don't get wet. | *Paula, no te mojes.* |
| Boys, don't get wet. | *Niños, no se mojen.* |
| Girls, try not to make a mess. | *Niñas, traten de no ensuciarlo todo.* |
| Paul, please don't get your shirt wet. | *Pablo, no te mojes la camisa, por favor.* |
| Victoria, do you want some lotion for your bottom? | *Victoria, ¿quieres crema para tu colita?* |

> **VOCABULARY NOTE**
>
> *Colita* is a nice word for bottom. If you must be more specific in referring to their "private parts," use *vagina* and *pene*, with a Spanish pronunciation. Not surprisingly, each region has its own slang for genitalia, but the above terms are generally understood and relatively neutral.

## Running hot and cold

| | |
|---|---|
| Henry, turn on the water. | *Enrique, abre el agua.*[1] |
| Olivia, will you turn on the hot water? | *Olivia, ¿quieres abrir el agua caliente?* |

---

1. *Agua* is feminine, but feminine nouns that begin with a stressed *a* in Spanish take a masculine article for phonetic reasons, just like we say "an apple" in English. Note that you would say "el agua fría," however.

| | |
|---|---|
| Is the water too cold? | *¿Está el agua demasiado fría?* |
| Paula, can you turn off the water? | *Paula, ¿puedes cerrar el agua?* |
| The water is running. | *El agua está corriendo.* |
| We are wasting water. | *Estamos desperdiciando agua.* |
| We don't want to waste water. | *No queremos desperdiciar agua.* |

## One, two, three little fingers

There is a little song that you can sing as your kids wash their hands with soap. This helps them get the soap all over and helps them to learn their numbers.

| | |
|---|---|
| One, two, three little fingers | *Uno, dos, tres deditos,* |
| Four, five, six little fingers | *Cuatro, cinco, seis deditos* |
| Seven, eight, nine little fingers | *Siete, ocho, nueve deditos* |
| And one little finger more makes ten. | *Y uno más son diez.* |

## BRUSHING TEETH

**KEY VOCABULARY:**

dental floss, *el hilo dental*
tooth, *el diente*
toothbrush, *el cepillo de dientes*
toothpaste, *la pasta de dientes,*
    *la pasta dentífrica*

to brush, *cepillar*
to open, *abrir*
to rinse, *enjuagar*

### Brushing teeth

When our kids were very young, we always brushed their teeth for them:

| | |
|---|---|
| Olivia, it is time to brush your teeth. | *Olivia, es hora de cepillarte los dientes.* |
| Olivia and Claire, let's brush our teeth. | *Olivia y Clara, vamos a cepillarnos los dientes.* |
| Edward, will you get me your toothbrush, please? | *Eduardo, ¿quieres buscarme tu cepillo de dientes, por favor?* |
| What color is your toothbrush? | *¿De qué color es tu cepillo de dientes?* |
| Sit on my lap. | *Siéntate en mi regazo.* |
| Put your head back. | *Haz la cabeza hacia atrás.* |
| Open your mouth, please. | *Abre la boca, por favor.* |
| Do you want water? | *¿Quieres agua?* |
| Rinse your mouth out. | *Enjuágate la boca.* |
| Don't swallow the toothpaste. | *No te tragues la pasta de dientes.* |
| Spit. | *Escupe.* |
| I'm going to floss you. | *Voy a limpiarte con hilo dental.* |
| Be still, please. | *Estate quieto, por favor.* |
| Done. | *Ya.* |

It wasn't long, of course, before they were doing it by themselves.

| | |
|---|---|
| Rachel, will you brush your teeth? | *Raquel, ¿quieres cepillarte los dientes?* |
| Boys, will you brush your teeth? | *Niños, ¿quieren cepillarse los dientes?* |
| Eve, where is your toothbrush? | *Eva, ¿dónde está tu cepillo de dientes?* |
| Where is the toothpaste? | *¿Dónde está la pasta de dientes?* |
| Charles, do not put a lot of toothpaste on your brush. | *Carlos, no le pongas mucha pasta al cepillo.* |

| | |
|---|---|
| Boys, do not put so much toothpaste on your brush. | *Niños, no le pongan tanta pasta al cepillo.* |
| Charles, spit in the sink, please. | *Carlos, escupe en el lavabo, por favor.* |
| Girls, spit in the sink. | *Niñas, escupan en el lavabo.* |
| Kids, did you clean all of your teeth? | *Niños, ¿se limpiaron todos los dientes?* |
| Olivia, did you clean your back teeth? | *Olivia, ¿te limpiaste los dientes de atrás?* |
| David and Adrian, did you clean your front teeth? | *David y Adrián, ¿se limpiaron los dientes de enfrente?* |
| Did you (all) brush well? | *¿Te cepillaste (Se cepillaron) bien?* |
| Boys, to avoid cavities it is important to brush your teeth every day. | *Niños, para evitar caries es importante cepillarse los dientes todos los días.* |

## Of teeth and tooth fairies

| | |
|---|---|
| You have a loose tooth. | *Tienes un diente flojo.* |
| It's very loose. | *Está muy flojo.* |
| Claire, are you losing a baby tooth? | *Clara, ¿estás perdiendo un diente de leche?* |
| You are getting a permanent tooth. | *Te está saliendo un diente permanente.* |
| Do you want to put it under your pillow for the tooth mouse? | *¿Quieres ponerlo debajo de tu almohada para el ratón de dientes?* |

### CULTURAL NOTE

In Latin America, it is the tooth mouse that brings money for teeth. In some places this mouse has a name, el ratón Pérez. If you want to say, literally, tooth fairy, say *el hada de dientes.*

# BATH AND BODY

**KEY VOCABULARY:**

ankle, *el tobillo*
arm, *el brazo*
cheek, *la mejilla*
chin, *la barbilla, el mentón*
ear (inner), *el oído*
ear (outer), *la oreja*
elbow, *el codo*
eye, *el ojo*
eyebrow, *la ceja*
eyelash, *la pestaña*
finger, *el dedo*
foot, *el pie*
forehead, *la frente*
hair, *el cabello, el pelo*
hand, *la mano*

head, *la cabeza*
heel, *el talón*
knee, *la rodilla*
leg, *la pierna*
lip, *el labio*
mouth, *la boca*
neck, *el cuello*
nose, *la nariz*
shoulder, *el hombro*
stomach (belly), *el estómago (la panza)*
thumb, *el pulgar*
tongue, *la lengua*
tooth, *el diente*
waist, *la cintura*
wrist, *la muñeca*

## Getting ready, getting in

Kids, it's bath time.
*Niños, es hora de bañarse.*

Henry, you have to take a bath now.
*Enrique, tienes que bañarte ahora.*

Girls, you have to take a shower.
*Niñas, tienen que ducharse.*

Henry, do you want to take a bath or a shower?
*Enrique, ¿quieres bañarte o ducharte?*

Let's turn on the water.
*Vamos a abrir el agua.*

Turn on the cold water first.
*Abre el agua fría primero.*

Let's fill the bathtub.
*Vamos a llenar la bañera.*

How is the water?
*¿Cómo está el agua?*

Is the water too hot?
*¿Está el agua demasiado caliente?*

Henry, turn off the hot water.
*Enrique, cierra el agua caliente.*

Is it too cold?
*¿Está demasiado fría?*

## Bathing and showering

Henry, you have to wash your hair today.
*Enrique, tienes que lavarte el pelo hoy.*

| | |
|---|---|
| Girls, you have to wash your hair today, too. | *Niñas, tienen que lavarse el pelo hoy también.* |
| Henry, do you want to do it by yourself, or do you want help? | *Enrique, ¿quieres hacerlo solo o quieres ayuda?* |
| Do you need soap? | *¿Necesitas jabón?* |
| Girls, do you need shampoo? | *Niñas, ¿necesitan champú?* |
| The container is empty? | *¿El envase está vacío?* |
| I'll get another one. | *Voy a buscar otro.* |
| Claire, is your hair wet? | *Clara, ¿tienes el pelo mojado?* |
| Let me help you. | *Déjame ayudarte.* |
| Olivia, close your eyes. | *Olivia, cierra los ojos.* |
| Did you get water in your eyes? | *¿Te entró agua en los ojos?* |
| Lucas, do you want a washcloth to cover your eyes? | *Lucas, ¿quieres una toallita para cubrirte los ojos?* |
| Girls, do you want to play for a few minutes? | *Niñas, ¿quieren jugar por unos cuantos minutos?* |
| Laura, do you want some bath toys? | *Laura, ¿quieres unos juguetes de baño?* |
| No splashing, please. | *No se chapotea, por favor.* |
| Lucas, you can play for five more minutes. | *Lucas, puedes jugar por cinco minutos más.* |
| Who wants to go out? | *¿Quién quiere salir?* |

## All clean!

| | |
|---|---|
| Laura, are you ready to get out? | *Laura, ¿estás lista para salir?* |
| Will you let the water out? | *¿Quieres dejar salir el agua?* |
| Adrian, please turn off the shower. | *Adrián, apaga la ducha, por favor.* |
| Boys, are you ready to dry off? | *Niños, ¿están listos para secarse?* |
| Laura, are you cold? | *Laura, ¿tienes frío?* |
| Lucas, here is a towel. | *Lucas, aquí tienes una toalla.* |
| Boys, can you hang your towels up after drying? | *Niños, pueden colgar las toallas después de secarse, por favor.* |
| Lucas, will you pick up your towel and put it in the bathroom? | *Lucas, ¿quieres recoger tu toalla y ponerla en el cuarto de baño?* |
| Laura, you need to dry your hair. | *Laura, tienes que secarte el pelo.* |
| I am going to get the hair dryer. | *Voy a buscar el secador de cabello.* |

# FEELINGS

## WHERE DOES IT HURT?

**KEY VOCABULARY:**

boo-boo, *una heridita (herida)*
bruise, *un moretón*
bump (swelling), *un chichón*
burn, *una quemadura*
cut, *una cortada*
hug, *un abrazo*
kiss, *un beso*
scrape, *una raspada*
a small bump on the head, *un coco*
    (short for *un coscorrón*)

to be itchy, *tener comezón*
to bump one's head, *darse un coco*
to burn (oneself), *quemar(se)*
to cut (oneself), *cortar(se)*
to fall (down), *caerse*
to trip (on), *tropezar (con)*

### Accidents will happen

Why are you crying?
Carla, tell me what happened.
Can someone tell me what happened?
Did you hurt yourself?
You have a boo-boo.
Did James hit his head?
Did he fall?

*¿Por qué estás llorando?*
*Carla, dime qué pasó.*
*¿Alguien puede decirme qué pasó?*
*¿Te heriste? ¿Te hiciste daño?*
*Tienes una heridita.*
*¿Se dio un coco Jaime?*
*¿Se cayó?*

| | |
|---|---|
| Did you fall off the swing? | *¿Te caíste del columpio?* |
| Did someone hit you? | *¿Te pegó alguien?* |
| Where did they hit you? | *¿Dónde te pegaron?* |
| The ball hit you. | *Te pegó la pelota.* |
| Did someone pinch you? | *¿Te pellizcó alguien?* |
| Did you catch your fingers in the door? | *¿Te cogiste los dedos en la puerta?* |
| Did Alexandra trip? | *¿Tropezó Alejandra?* |
| Alexandra tripped on a rock. | *Alejandra tropezó con una piedra.* |

## Where does it hurt?

| | |
|---|---|
| Carla, tell me, where does it hurt? | *Carla, dime, ¿dónde te duele?* |
| Show me where it hurts. | *Enséñame dónde te duele.* |
| Does your head hurt? | *¿Te duele la cabeza?* |
| Do your knees hurt? | *¿Te duelen las rodillas?* |

See the glossary for other body parts.

| | |
|---|---|
| You have a bruise on your arm. | *Tienes un moretón en el brazo.* |
| Did you scrape your knee? | *¿Te raspaste la rodilla?* |
| You have a scrape on your knee. | *Tienes una raspada en la rodilla.* |
| Your knee is bleeding. | *La rodilla te está sangrando.* |
| Adrian's nose is bleeding. | *La nariz le está sangrando a Adrián.* |
| Did Teresa cut her hand? | *¿Se cortó la mano Teresa?* |
| She has a cut on her leg. | *Tiene una cortada en la pierna.* |
| You have a little cut on your finger. | *Tienes una cortadita en el dedo.* |
| You have a bump on your head. | *Tienes un coco en la cabeza.* |
| Your ankle is swollen. | *Tienes hinchado el tobillo.* |
| Your wrist is swollen. | *Tienes hinchada la muñeca.* |
| Did you burn yourself? | *¿Te quemaste?* |
| Did something sting you? | *¿Te picó algo?* |
| A mosquito bit you. | *Te picó un mosquito (un zancudo).* |
| You have a mosquito bite. | *Tienes una picadura de mosquito (zancudo).* |
| | |
| Does your leg itch? | *¿Te pica la pierna?* |
| Does your hand feel itchy? | *¿Tienes comezón en la mano?* |
| Try not to scratch. | *Trata de no rascarte.* |

## Making boo-boos better

| | |
|---|---|
| Let's wash your boo-boo. | *Vamos a lavar tu heridita.* |
| Do you want a Band-Aid? | *¿Quieres una curita?* |
| Do you want to put ice on your bump? | *¿Quieres ponerte hielo en el chichón?* |
| Would you like a little medicine? | *¿Quieres un poco de medicina?* |

---

**VOCABULARY NOTE**

In Mexico, a bump is also *un chipote*. A cloth bandage is *una venda*.

---

Of course, the traditional remedies are often all that is needed:

| | |
|---|---|
| Sara, do you want a kiss? | *Sara, ¿quieres un beso?* |
| Let me kiss your boo-boo and make it better. | *Déjame besarte la heridita y hacerla sanar.* |
| Let me give you a hug. | *Déjame darte un abrazo.* |
| Are you better now? | *¿Ya estás mejor?* |

The following Spanish remedy works wonders. Simply rub the boo-boo with your hand and recite:

| | |
|---|---|
| Get well, get well, little frog tail, | *Sana, sana, colita de rana.* |
| If you don't today, tomorrow you will. | *Si no sanas hoy, sanarás mañana.* |

## Cold season

Unfortunately, kids get sick, even in Spanish.

| | |
|---|---|
| Alexandra, how do you feel? | *Alejandra, ¿cómo te sientes?* |
| Do you feel well (bad)? | *¿Te sientes bien (mal)?* |
| Ernest, are you sick? | *Ernesto, ¿estás enfermo?* |
| Claire is a little sick. | *Clara está enfermita.* |
| She has a runny nose. | *Tiene la nariz floja.* |
| Blow your nose. | *Suénate la nariz. (Límpiate la nariz.)* |
| Does something hurt? | *¿Algo te duele?* |
| What hurts? | *¿Qué te duele?* |

| | |
|---|---|
| Does your head (stomach, ear) hurt? | *¿Te duele la cabeza (el estómago, el oído)?* |
| Which ear hurts? | *¿Qué oído te duele?* |
| Mark, point to where it hurts. | *Marcos, señala dónde te duele.* |
| Are you hot? Are you cold? | *¿Tienes calor? ¿Tienes frío?* |
| Do you have chills? | *¿Tienes escalofríos?* |
| You have goose bumps. | *Se te hace la piel de gallina.* |
| You are sweating. | *Estás sudando.* |
| Let me feel your forehead. | *Déjame tocarte la frente.* |
| We have to take your temperature. | *Tenemos que tomarte la temperatura.* |
| Put the thermometer under your arm (tongue). | *Ponte el termómetro debajo del brazo (de la lengua).* |
| You seem hot. | *Parece que tienes calor.* |
| You have a fever. | *Tienes fiebre.* |
| Do you have nausea? | *¿Tienes náuseas?* |
| Do you feel like throwing up? | *¿Tienes ganas de vomitar?* |
| Are you going to vomit? | *¿Vas a vomitar?* |
| Do you have to go to the bathroom? | *¿Tienes que ir al baño?* |
| Do you have diarrhea? | *¿Tienes diarrea?* |

## The diagnosis

| | |
|---|---|
| You have a cold. | *Tienes un resfriado.* |
| You have the flu. | *Tienes gripe.* |
| You have an ear infection. | *Tienes una infección de oído.* |
| You have the chicken pox. | *Tienes varicela.* |

## Taking your medicine

| | |
|---|---|
| It is time to take your medicine. | *Es hora de tomar tu medicina.* |
| James, do you want to do it by yourself? | *Jaime, ¿quieres hacerlo solo?* |
| Ana, can you take your medicine by yourself? | *Ana, ¿puedes tomar la medicina sola?* |
| The medicine is going to make you get better. | *La medicina te va a curar.* |
| The medicine is going to help you to feel better. | *La medicina te va a ayudar a sentirte mejor.* |

| | |
|---|---|
| The medicine is going to help you to fall asleep. | *La medicina te va a ayudar a dormirte.* |
| Would you like some water with your medicine? | *¿Quieres un poco de agua con tu medicina?* |
| Would you like some applesauce or some soup with crackers? | *¿Quieres puré de manzana o sopa con galletas saladas?* |
| Try to eat a little bit. | *Trata de comer un poco.* |
| Would you like to lie on the sofa and watch television? | *¿Te gustaría acostarte en el sofá y ver la televisión?* |

## EMOTIONS

|  |  |
|---|---|
| Paula, what's the matter? | Paula, ¿qué te pasa? |
| Boys, what's the matter? | Niños, ¿qué les pasa? |
| Girls, are you happy? | Niñas, ¿están contentas? |
| Jude, are you sad? | Judas, ¿estás triste? |
| Paul, tell me why you are sad. | Pablo, dime por qué estás triste. |
| Boys, are you angry? | Niños, ¿están enojados? |
| Boys, tell me why you are angry. | Niños, díganme, ¿por qué están enojados? |
| Claire, did someone hurt your feelings? | Clara, ¿alguien te hizo sentir mal? |
| Martha, did you hurt Claire's feelings? | Marta, ¿le hiciste sentir mal a Clara? |
| Daniel, are you crying? | Daniel, ¿estás llorando? |
| Why are you crying? | ¿Por qué estás llorando? |
| Michael, are you afraid? | Miguel, ¿tienes miedo? |
| Boys, are you afraid? | Niños, ¿tienen miedo? |
| Jane, did you get scared? | Juana, ¿te asustaste? |
| What scared you? | ¿Qué te asustó? |
| Boys, what scared you? | Niños, ¿qué los asustó? |
| Saraí, what are you afraid of? | Saraí, ¿qué te da miedo? |
| Boys, what are you afraid of? | Niños, ¿qué les da miedo? |
| There is nothing to fear. | No hay nada que temer. |
| Martha, tell your sister you're sorry. | Marta, dile a tu hermana que lo sientes. |
| | Marta, discúlpate con tu hermana. |
| Martha and John, tell the other kids you are sorry. | Marta y Juan, díganles a los otros niños que lo sienten. |
| Do you (all) miss daddy? | ¿Extrañas (Extrañan) a papi? |
| | ¿Echas (Echan) de menos a papi? |
| Clara, I am going to miss you. | Clara, voy a extrañarte. |
| Boys, I am going to miss you. | Niños, voy a extrañarlos. |

# FAMILY AND FRIENDS

## FAMILY

### Kids

A little girl is *una niña*, and a little boy is *un niño*. Little boys and girls, taken together, are *los niños*. Little girls, as a group, are *las niñas*.

El Niño, the meteorological phenomenon during which the waters of the Pacific heat up and wreak havoc on the world's weather patterns, is named after the Christ child because the phenomenon commences around Christmastime.

You also may have heard the terms *muchacho* and *muchacha*, which simply mean *boy* and *girl*, respectively. Often these are applied to older kids. Colloquially, you may also hear *chico* and *chica*.

### The immediate family

| | |
|---|---|
| dad | *papá* |
| daddy | *papi* |
| daughter | *hija* |
| family | *la familia* |
| father | *padre* |
| mom | *mamá* |
| mommy | *mami* |
| mother | *madre* |
| son | *hijo* |

In practice, you do not hear *padre* or *madre* very much. (*Madre* is almost a swearword in some countries and in some contexts for reasons we will not go into right now.) *Mamá*, *papá*, *mami*, and *papi* are very common. By the way, the word for *parents* is *padres* or *papás*. The word *parientes* means *relatives*.

| | |
|---|---|
| brother | *hermano* |
| sister | *hermana* |
| brothers and sisters | *hermanos* |
| older brother | *hermano mayor* |
| older sister | *hermana mayor* |
| younger brother | *hermano menor, hermanito* |
| younger sister | *hermana menor, hermanita* |

## The extended family

Most of us have some contact with our extended family. In most Hispanic cultures, extended family still plays an important role in the raising of kids.

| | |
|---|---|
| grandfather | *abuelo* |
| grandmother | *abuela* |
| grandparents | *abuelos* |
| grandson | *nieto* |
| granddaughter | *nieta* |
| grandsons | *nietos* |
| granddaughters | *nietas* |
| grandchildren (of both sexes) | *nietos* |
| uncle | *tío* |
| aunt | *tía* |
| uncles | *tíos* |
| aunts | *tías* |
| aunts and uncles | *tíos* |
| nephew | *sobrino* |
| niece | *sobrina* |
| nephews | *sobrinos* |
| nieces | *sobrinas* |
| nieces and nephews | *sobrinos* |
| boy cousin | *primo* |
| girl cousin | *prima* |
| cousins (boys or mixed) | *primos* |
| girl cousins | *primas* |

Note that when talking about cousins you use *primos* unless all of them happen to be female, in which case you would use *primas*. For example, suppose that you are going to your sister's house and that she has a boy and a girl. These are your kids' *primos*. If, on the other hand, your sister has two girls, then you are going to visit the kids' *primas*. (As you have seen, this same rule applies to *hermanos, tíos, abuelos*, etc.)

| | |
|---|---|
| godfather | *padrino* |
| godmother | *madrina* |
| godparents | *padrinos* |

If Bob and June are the godparents of your child, then Bob and June are your *compadres*; they are your "co-parents." Specifically, Bob is your *compadre* and June is your *comadre*.

Finally, for reasons of death and divorce, kids could have stepparents, stepbrothers, stepsisters, half sisters, and half brothers.

| | |
|---|---|
| stepfather | *padrastro* |
| stepmother | *madrastra* |
| stepparents | *padrastros* |
| stepbrother | *hermanastro* |
| stepsister | *hermanastra* |
| half brother | *medio hermano* |
| half sister | *media hermana* |
| stepson | *hijastro* |
| stepdaughter | *hijastra* |

And let us not forget the in-laws.

| | |
|---|---|
| father-in-law | *suegro* |
| mother-in-law | *suegra* |
| brother-in-law | *cuñado* |
| sister-in-law | *cuñada* |

## Describing relationships

Kids are fascinated by relationships. At a recent wedding, Claire (Steve and Mary's daughter) insisted on spending the bulk of the evening dancing with her godfather even though we had not seen him in a long time. (He lives in Alaska.)

Explaining relationships in Spanish is fairly straightforward and, for the most part, corresponds to the explanations that you might give in English. As usual, you must take into account whether you are speaking to one child or to several children. (We will use the awkward but understandable *you all's* to indicate this.)

| | |
|---|---|
| Bobby is your (you all's) cousin. | *Bobby es tu (su) primo.* |
| Sally is your (you all's) cousin. | *Sally es tu (su) prima.* |
| Doug is your (you all's) uncle. | *Doug es tu (su) tío.* |
| Mary is your (you all's) aunt. | *María es tu (su) tía.* |
| Dave and Mike are your (you all's) uncles. | *Dave y Mike son tus (sus) tíos.* |

If you are a fairly typical family, chances are that at least some of your close relatives are not so close geographically. Where, then, do they live?

| | |
|---|---|
| Your (you all's) uncle Doug lives in California. | *Tu (Su) tío Doug vive en California.* |
| Your (you all's) grandparents live in New York. | *Tus (Sus) abuelos viven en Nueva York.* |

You will also want to explain to your kids the relationships of their aunts, uncles, grandparents, etc. to you.

| | |
|---|---|
| Jeff is my brother. | *Jeff es mi hermano.* |
| Andrea is my sister. | *Andrea es mi hermana.* |
| Dave is Daddy's brother. | *Dave es el hermano de papi.* |
| Lisa is Mommy's sister. | *Lisa es la hermana de mami.* |
| Grandfather Clarkie is my father. | *Tu abuelo Clarkie es mi papá.* |
| Grandmother Barb is Mommy's mother. | *Tu abuela Barb es la mamá de mami.* |

## Terms of endearment

There are many terms of endearment, and often it is difficult to give a translation that gives the exact feeling. Most would be replaced by *dear* in English. Here are a few:

| | |
|---|---|
| *Mi hijo. Mi hija.* | My son. My daughter. Also, the diminutives: *Mi hijito, mi hijita.* |

| | |
|---|---|
| *Mi cielo.* | *Cielo* means *sky* or *heaven*. Note that the same word is used for both boys and girls. "Cielito lindo" is the title of a famous Mexican song that refers to a little girl. |
| *Cariño* | *Cariño* literally means affection. Again, it is the same for boys and girls. |
| *Querido. Querida.* | Dear. |
| *Mi amor.* | My love. |
| *Tesoro.* | Treasure. |

# DESCRIBING PEOPLE

### KEY VOCABULARY: ATTRIBUTES

**A few physical traits**
big, *grande*
blond, *rubio*
brunette, *castaño*
curly hair, *el pelo rizado*
fat, *gordo*
gray hair, *el pelo cano*
long (short) hair, *el pelo largo (corto)*
old, *viejo, mayor*
redheaded, *pelirrojo*
short, *bajo*
small, *pequeño*
straight hair, *el pelo liso*
tall, *alto*
thin, *delgado, flaco*
young, *joven*

**Personality traits**
bossy, *mandón, mandona*
bright, clever, *listo*
disagreeable, *antipático*
friendly, *amigable, amistoso*
fun, *divertido*
funny, *chistoso*
kind, *amable*
nice, *simpático*
playful, *juguetón, juguetona*
smart, *inteligente*

### KEY VOCABULARY: PROFESSIONS

actor, actress, *el actor, la actriz*
architect, *el arquitecto, la arquitecta*
artist, *el artista, la artista*
baseball player, *el jugador /*
    *la jugadora de béisbol*
biologist, *el biólogo, la bióloga*
businessman/woman, *el hombre /*
    *la mujer de negocios*
doctor (medical), *el médico,*
    *el doctor, la doctora*
engineer, *el ingeniero, la ingeniera*
firefighter, *el bombero, la bombera*
guard, *el guardia, la guardia*
guide, *el guía, la guía*
lawyer, *el abogado, la abogada*
merchant, *el comerciante,*
    *la comerciante*

minister (religious), *el pastor, la pastora*
movie star, *la estrella de cine*
    (masculine or feminine)
philosopher, *el filósofo, la filósofa*
pianist, *el pianista, la pianista*
plumber, *el plomero, la plomera*
poet, *el poeta, la poeta*
policeman, woman, *el policía, la policía*
politician, *el político, la política*
president, *el presidente, la presidenta*
priest, *el sacerdote, la sacerdote*
professor, *el profesor, la profesora*
sales clerk, *el dependiente,*
    *la dependiente*
salesperson, *el vendedor, la vendedora*
sales representative, *el representante,*
    *la representante*

senator, *el senador, la senadora*
singer, *el cantante, la cantante*
soccer player, *el futbolista,*
    *la futbolista, el jugador de fútbol,*
    *la jugadora de fútbol*

sociologist, *el sociólogo, la socióloga*
teacher, *el maestro, la maestra*

## Describing people: "Five foot two . . ."

The following are phrases to describe people. Keep in mind that the adjectives must reflect the number and gender of the person or persons described.

| | |
|---|---|
| Paul is tall. | *Pablo es alto.* |
| Andrea is tall. | *Andrea es alta.* |
| Paul and Andrea are tall. | *Pablo y Andrea son altos.* |
| Mary and Andrea are tall. | *María y Andrea son altas.* |
| Andrea is short. | *Andrea es baja.* |
| Paul is fat. | *Pablo es gordo.* |
| Mary is thin. | *María es delgada.* |
| The sisters are skinny. | *Las hermanas son flacas.* |

---

**VOCABULARY NOTE**

Although *grande* and *pequeño* are sometimes used to refer to age, more often they refer to size. You can usually tell by the context.

*Bajo* means short in stature (also *bajito, chaparrito*). Short in length or short in time would be *corto*.

---

| | |
|---|---|
| He is big for his age. | *Es grande para su edad.* |
| The boys are small for their ages. | *Los niños son pequeños para su edad.* |

## Eyes of blue

| | |
|---|---|
| Nuria has blue eyes. | *Nuria tiene los ojos azules.* |
| She has short hair. | *Tiene el pelo corto.* |
| Alfredo has curly hair. | *Alfredo tiene el pelo rizado.* |
| They have blond hair. | *Tienen el pelo rubio.* |

| | |
|---|---|
| Her mother has brunette hair. | *Su mamá tiene el pelo castaño.* |
| My father has long black hair. | *Mi papá tiene el pelo negro y largo.* |
| The redheaded girls are coming to visit us. | *Las niñas pelirrojas van a venir a visitarnos.* |
| The boy with the green eyes is coming to play. | *El niño de los ojos verdes viene a jugar.* |
| The blonde woman is Mary's mother. | *La rubia es la mamá de María.* |
| My uncle has gray hair. | *Mi tío tiene el pelo cano.* |

## People I like . . . and why

In English we distinguish between *to like* and *to love*. In Spanish we can make the same distinction. To love is *querer*. The best way to express *to like* is to use *caer* (to fall). Literally, someone is "falling well to us." The use of *caer* is a bit tricky. The following examples should give you the hang of it. (If you are used to using *gustar*, then this will be no problem for you.)

| | |
|---|---|
| Patricia, do you like Tom? | *Patricia, ¿te cae bien Tomás?* |
| Girls, do you like Tom? | *Niñas, ¿les cae bien Tomás?* |
| Yes, we like him. | *Sí, nos cae bien.* |
| No, we don't like him. | *No, no nos cae bien. Nos cae mal.* |
| Patricia, do like the boys? | *Patricia, ¿te caen bien los niños?* |
| Girls, do you like the boys? | *Niñas, ¿les caen bien los niños?* |
| Daniela, how do you like your teacher? | *Daniela, ¿cómo te cae tu maestra?* |
| I like her a lot. | *Me cae muy bien.* |
| She's OK. | *Me cae regular.* |
| I like them a lot. | *Me caen muy bien.* |

Love is another matter . . . although for kids it may not be.

| | |
|---|---|
| I love you. | *Te quiero.* |
| I love my teacher. | *Quiero a mi maestra.* |
| Gabriel, your grandmother really loves you. | *Gabriel, tu abuela te quiere mucho.* |
| I know that you love her too. | *Sé que tú la quieres también.* |
| Kids, I can see that you love your grandparents. | *Niños, puedo ver que quieren a sus abuelos.* |

---

**VOCABULARY NOTE**

Note that *amar* and *querer* mean *to love*. *Quiero a mi maestro* means *I love (am in love with) my teacher*. To say "I like my teacher," you might use *Me cae bien mi maestro*; for "I really like my teacher," use *Me encanta mi maestro*. Avoid using *gustar* with people as this may (in some countries) have a sexual connotation.

---

You can use *parecer* to ask your kids what someone is like or what they think about him or her.

| | |
|---|---|
| John, what do you think of your cousin? | *Juan, ¿qué te parece tu primo?* |
| John and Mary, what do you think about your aunt? | *Juan y María, ¿qué les parece su tía?* |
| I like her. | *Me cae bien.* |
| She seems nice. | *Me parece simpática.* |

Kids (and other people) can have all sorts of positive characteristics:

| | |
|---|---|
| Mary is very intelligent. | *María es muy inteligente.* |
| Paul is very bright. | *Pablo es muy listo.* |
| Victor is very playful. | *Víctor es muy juguetón.* |
| Ellen is very playful too. | *Elena es muy juguetona también.* |
| Maya is very fun. | *Maya es muy divertida.* |
| Tom is very funny. | *Tomás es muy chistoso.* |
| The boys are nice. | *Los niños son simpáticos.* |
| The girls are friendly. | *Las niñas son amigables.* |
| They are very kind. | *Son muy amables.* |

Or not so positive:

| | |
|---|---|
| The boys are very mischievous. | *Los niños son muy traviesos.* |
| Paul, don't be so bossy. | *Pablo, no seas tan mandón.* |
| Angela is very bossy. | *Ángela es muy mandona.* |
| John and Martha, don't be tattletales. | *Juan y Marta, no sean soplones.* |

## How old are you?

In Spanish, age is something that you have. (Or rather, *years* are something you have.)

| | |
|---|---|
| Siena, how old are you? | *Siena, ¿cuántos años tienes?* |
| Aida and Olivia, how old are you? | *Aída y Olivia, ¿cuántos años tienen?* |

Sooner or later, your kids are going to ask you how old you are and you are going to have to fess up:

| | |
|---|---|
| I am forty-two years old. | *Tengo cuarenta y dos años.* |

This brings us to the word *old*. In Spanish, the word *viejo* is generally applied only to old people or old things. Thus:

| | |
|---|---|
| Your grandfather is very old. | *Tu abuelo es muy viejo.* |
| You all's great-grandmother is very old. | *Su bisabuela es muy vieja.* |

Kids are never old, no matter how fast they seem to grow up. After a kid tells you his or her age, you might reply:

| | |
|---|---|
| How big you are! | *¡Qué mayor eres!* |

In Spanish, you would not say, *¡Qué viejo eres!*, even though in English you could say, How old you are! Likewise if you were talking to two kids and you wanted to know which was older, you would not say, *¿Quién es más viejo?*, but rather:

| | |
|---|---|
| Who is older? | *¿Quién es mayor?* |

It is, of course, very common to want to comment on perceived changes:

| | |
|---|---|
| Roberto, you're getting so big (tall)! | *Roberto, ¡qué grande (alto) te estás poniendo!* |
| Alicia, your hair is getting so long! | *Alicia, se te está poniendo tan largo el pelo.* |

## VISITS AND SLEEPOVERS

**KEY VOCABULARY:**

house, *la casa*
to remember, *recordar*
to take, *llevar*

to spend the night, *pasar la noche*
to behave, *portarse bien*

### Going to someone's house

Going to someone's house has a little different construction than in English. You don't go to *Mary's house*. Rather you go to the *house of Mary*. Likewise, you don't go to *the Smiths' house* but rather to the *house of the Smith*. (When referring to a family, the last name is singular but the definite article is plural: *los Smith*.) Note also that, in Spanish, you go to the house of *the* Mrs. Smith. A definite article precedes all titles (with the exception of *Don* and *Doña*, denoting the utmost respect) unless you are speaking directly to the person with the title.

Let's go to Mary's house.
*Vamos a la casa de María.*

Let's go to Mrs. Smith's house.
*Vamos a la casa de la señora Smith.*

Let's go to the Smiths' house.
*Vamos a la casa de los Smith.*

Mr. Smith, we are going to your house tomorrow.
*Señor Smith, vamos a su casa mañana.*

### Sleepovers

Sleepovers are great fun for kids.

John, do you want to spend the night at Peter's house?
*Juan, ¿quieres pasar la noche en casa de Pedro?*

Olivia and Claire, do you want to spend the night at Mary's house?
*Olivia y Clara, ¿quieren pasar la noche en casa de María?*

John, do want to sleep over at Peter's house?
*Juan, ¿quieres dormir en casa de Pedro?*

Saraí and Claire, do you want to sleep over at Mary's house?
*Saraí y Clara, ¿quieren dormir en casa de María?*

John, take your toothbrush.
*Juan, llévate el cepillo de dientes.*

| | |
|---|---|
| Saraí and Claire, take some clothes for the morning. | *Saraí y Clara, lleven ropa para la mañana.* |
| John, do you want to take your teddy bear? | *Juan, ¿quieres llevar tu oso de peluche?* |
| Olivia and Saraí, do you want to take some books? | *Olivia y Saraí, ¿quieren llevar unos libros?* |
| John, remember that you must behave. | *Juan, recuerda que tienes que portarte bien.* |
| You must listen to Peter's mother. | *Tienes que escucharle a la mamá de Pedro.* |
| You must go to bed when Peter's mother tells you to. | *Tienes que acostarte cuando te diga la mamá de Pedro.* |
| Saraí and Claire, remember that you must behave. | *Saraí y Clara, recuerden que tienen que portarse bien.* |
| You (all) must listen to Mary's mother. | *Tienen que escucharle a la mamá de María.* |
| You (all) must go to bed when Mary's mother says. | *Tienen que irse a la cama cuando les diga la mamá de María.* |
| Behave yourself. | *Pórtate bien.* |
| Behave yourselves. | *Pórtense bien.* |

## Saying goodbye

In Spanish, as in English, there are many ways to say goodbye. We will give the (more or less) literal translations in English so you can understand the differences.

| | |
|---|---|
| Goodbye! | *¡Adiós!* |
| Until later! | *¡Hasta luego!* |
| Until soon! | *¡Hasta pronto!* |
| Until we see each other. | *¡Hasta la vista!* |
| We'll see each other! | *¡Nos vemos!* |

One of the difficulties of a successful visit or sleepover is getting your kids to say goodbye.

| | |
|---|---|
| Lisa, it is time for us to leave. | *Lisa, es hora de irnos.* |
| John, say goodbye to your friends. | *Juan, diles adiós a tus amigos.* |
| John and Elsa, say goodbye to Grace. | *Juan y Elsa, díganle adiós a Graciela.* |

| | |
|---|---|
| Mary, give Martha a hug and tell her goodbye. | *María, dale un abrazo a Marta y dile adiós.* |

In Spanish the verb *despedirse* is very commonly used and means "to take leave" or "to see off." It is probably best translated as "to say goodbye."

| | |
|---|---|
| Jude, say goodbye to your friends. | *Judas, despídete de tus amigos.* |
| Jude and Elsa, say goodbye to Grace. | *Judas y Elsa, despídanse de Graciela.* |

And this is good time to remind them to say "thank you."

| | |
|---|---|
| Jude, say thank you to Paul and his parents for having you over. | *Judas, diles gracias a Pablo y a sus papás por haberte invitado.* |
| Jude and Elsa, tell them thanks for taking you to the movies. | *Judas y Elsa, díganles gracias por haberlos llevado al cine.* |

# OUR ANIMAL FRIENDS

Animals make up an important part of many children's lives, from pets to characters in stories to visits to the zoo. This chapter is mostly vocabulary, but it is vocabulary well worth learning. (You may be surprised by how often animals do come up.)

## PETS, *LAS MASCOTAS*

cat, *el gato*
dog, *el perro*
guinea pig, *el cuy*

hamster, *el hámster*
mouse, *el ratón*
parakeet, *el periquito*

## CARING FOR PETS, *CUIDANDO DE LAS MASCOTAS*

bowl, *el bol*
collar, *el collar*
kennel (portable kind), *la jaula*
leash, *la correa*

to brush, *cepillar*
to feed, *darle de comer*
to pick up (poop), *recoger (la caquita)*
to take out, *sacar*
to walk, *pasear*

## FARM ANIMALS, *ANIMALES DE LA GRANJA*

bull, *el toro*
chick, *el pollito*
chicken, *el pollo*
cow, *la vaca*
duck, *el pato*
ducklings, *los patitos*
goat, *el chivo, la cabra*

hen, *la gallina*
horse, *el caballo*
pig, *el puerco, el cochino*
rooster, *el gallo*
sheep, *la oveja*
turkey, *el pavo*

## WILD ANIMALS, *ANIMALES EN LA NATURALEZA*

alligator, *el caimán*[1]
bat, *el murciélago*
bear, *el oso*
beaver, *el castor*
camel, *el camello*

crocodile, *el cocodrilo*
deer, *el ciervo, el venado*
dolphin, *el delfín*
elephant, *el elefante*
fish, *el pez*

---

1. The English word *alligator* actually comes from the Spanish *el lagarto*, large lizard.

frog, *la rana*
   tadpole, *el renacuajo*
giraffe, *la jirafa*
hippopotamus, *el hipopótamo*
jellyfish, *la medusa*
lion, *el león*
lizard, *la lagartija*
monkey, *el mono*
   small monkey, *el chango*
mouse, *un ratón*
otter, *la nutria*

rabbit, *el conejo*
rat, *la rata*
rhinoceros, *el rinoceronte*
shark, *el tiburón*
skunk, *el zorrillo, la mofeta*
snake, *la serpiente, la culebra*
squirrel, *la ardilla*
tiger, *el tigre*
whale, *la ballena*
zebra, *la cebra*

## BIRDS, *LOS PÁJAROS*

bluebird, *el azulejo*
eagle, *el águila (f)*
falcon, *el halcón*
owl, *el búho*
penguin, *el pingüino*

robin, *el petirrojo*
swallow, *la golondrina*
sparrow, *el gorrión*
stork, *la cigüeña*
woodpecker, *el pájaro carpintero*

## INSECTS (BUGS), *INSECTOS (BICHOS)*

ant, *la hormiga*
bee, *la abeja*
beetle, *el escarabajo*
butterfly, *la mariposa*
centipede, *el ciempiés*
cricket, *el grillo*
dragonfly, *la libélula*
firefly, *la luciérnaga*
fly, *la mosca*

grasshopper, *el saltamontes*
ladybug, *la mariquita*
mosquito, *el mosquito*
scorpion, *el alacrán*
spider, *la araña*
wasp, *la avispa*
worm, *el gusano*
   earthworm, *la lombriz*

## Animal talk

It's interesting to see the sounds that animals make in other languages. Here are some common ones in Spanish:

| | |
|---|---|
| The dog barks. | *El perro ladra.* |
| The cat meows and purrs. | *El gato maúlla y ronronea.* |
| The horse neighs. | *El caballo relincha.* |
| The frog croaks. | *La rana croa.* |
| The bird chirps. | *El pájaro trina.* |
| The cow moos. | *La vaca muge.* |
| The sheep baas. | *La oveja bala.* |
| The chick peeps. | *El pollito pía.* |
| The lion roars. | *El león ruge.* |
| The snake hisses. | *La serpiente sisea.* |
| The pig oinks. | *El cerdo gruñe.* |
| The hen clucks. | *La gallina cacarea.* |
| The rooster crows. | *El gallo canta.* |
| The donkey brays. | *El burro rebuzna.* |
| The duck quacks. | *El pato grazna.* |
| The dove coos. | *La paloma arrulla.* |
| The bee buzzes. | *La abeja zumba.* |

## Animals at home

A female cat is *una gata*, and a female dog is *una perra*.

| | |
|---|---|
| Adrian, have you fed the cat? | *Adrián, ¿le has dado de comer al gato?* |
| Does he have water? | *¿Tiene agua?* |
| Alexandra, you have to walk the dog this afternoon. | *Alejandra, tienes que pasear al perro esta tarde.* |
| Take Bea out. | *Saca a Bea.* |
| Get her collar and leash. | *Busca su collar y correa.* |
| Take a bag with you to pick up his poop. | *Lleva una bolsa contigo para recoger la caquita.* |
| Take his ball, and you can throw it for him in the park. | *Lleva su pelota y puedes tirársela en el parque.* |
| Alexandra and Adrian, you need to clean the hamsters' cage. | *Alejandra y Adrián, tienen que limpiar la jaula de los hámsteres.* |
| Do they have food? | *¿Tienen comida?* |

# BEHAVING AND MANNERS

## GETTING ALONG

**KEY VOCABULARY:**

mischief, *una travesura*
mischievous, *travieso*
permission, *el permiso*

to behave, *portarse bien*
to bite, *morder*
to bother, *molestar*
to cooperate, *cooperar*
to hit, *pegar*

to include, *incluir*
to leave alone, *dejar en paz*
to listen, *escuchar*
to pinch, *pellizcar*
to push, *empujar*
to shout, *gritar*
to take care of, *cuidar*
to take turns, *turnarse*

### Behaving, listening, and cooperating

Behave yourself (yourselves).
Do not (you all) make mischief.
Julie, listen, please.
Kids, listen to me.
Julie, are you going to cooperate
with me this morning?
Kids, are you going to cooperate so
that we can go to the zoo?

*Pórtate (Pórtense) bien.*
*No hagas (hagan) travesuras.*
*Julia, escucha, por favor.*
*Niños, escúchenme.*
*Julia, ¿vas a cooperar conmigo esta*
*mañana?*
*Niños, ¿van a cooperar para que*
*podamos ir al zoológico?*

| | |
|---|---|
| You all have to cooperate if you want to go to the park. | *Tienen que cooperar si quieren ir al parque.* |

And the ubiquitous "Stop right there!"

| | |
|---|---|
| James, stop! | *Jaime, ¡para!* |
| Kids, stop immediately! | *Niños, ¡paren enseguida!* |
| Andrea, stop hitting immediately. | *Andrea, ¡para de pegar ya!* |

## Including others

| | |
|---|---|
| Olivia, you have to take care of your little sister. | *Olivia, tienes que cuidar a tu hermanita.* |
| Olivia, you have to include Claire. | *Olivia, tienes que incluir a Clara.* |
| Olivia and Siena, you have to include John. | *Olivia y Siena, tienen que incluir a Juan.* |
| Juan, will you please play with your little brother? | *Juan, ¿quieres jugar con tu hermanito, por favor?* |

## Leaving others alone

Sometimes it is just enough to get one kid to leave another alone.

| | |
|---|---|
| John, don't bother your sister. | *Juan, no molestes a tu hermana.* |
| Girls, don't bother your little brother. | *Niñas, no molesten a su hermanito.* |
| John, leave your sister alone. | *Juan, deja en paz a tu hermana.* |
| Girls, leave your little brother alone. | *Niñas, dejen en paz a su hermanito.* |
| Eve, leave him alone. | *Eva, déjalo en paz.* |
| Boys, leave her alone. | *Niños, déjenla en paz.* |
| Rachel, let your sister do it by herself. | *Raquel, deja que tu hermana lo haga sola.* |
| Rachel, let her do it by herself. | *Raquel, deja que lo haga sola.* |

## Sharing and taking turns

| | |
|---|---|
| We have to take turns. | *Tenemos que turnarnos.* |
| You all have to take turns. | *Tienen que turnarse.* |
| Isabel and Joseph, you have to take turns. | *Isabel y José, tienen que turnarse.* |

The most natural way to indicate whose turn it is in Spanish is with the verb *tocar*. *Me toca* (It's my turn) literally means "It touches me."

| Whose turn is it? | *¿A quién le toca?* |
| It is my turn. | *Me toca (a mí).* |
| It is Paul's turn. | *Le toca a Pablo.* |
| It is Mary and Sarah's turn. | *Les toca a María y Sara.* |
| It is my turn to dance. | *A mí me toca bailar.* |
| It is Paul's turn to play with the train. | *A Pablo le toca jugar con el tren.* |

You also hear the following expressions:

| It's my turn. | *Es mi turno.* |
| It's Paul's turn. | *Es el turno de Pablo.* |

You may want to explain why it is someone else's turn, or you may want to set some ground rules for sharing.

| You have had the doll for a long time already. | *Ya llevas mucho tiempo con la muñeca.* |
| You have been playing on the computer for a long time already. | *Ya llevas mucho tiempo jugando en la computadora.* |
| You had it for a long time. | *Ya llevas mucho tiempo con él (ella).*[1] |
| You can play with it for ten minutes and then it is John's turn. | *Puedes jugar con él (ella) por diez minutos y después le toca a Juan.* |
| Each person can have a turn of five minutes. | *Cada persona puede tener un turno de cinco minutos.* |

## The no-no's and other rules

| That is not done. (You shouldn't do that.) | *Eso no se hace.* |
| What are the rules? | *¿Cuáles son las reglas?* |
| Who can tell me a rule for playing? | *¿Quién puede decirme una regla para jugar?* |
| No hitting. | *No se pega.* |

---

1. You would use *él* if you are talking about something masculine such as a boat (*el barco*) and *ella* if you are talking about something feminine such as a computer (*la computadora*).

| | |
|---|---|
| No biting. | *No se muerde.* |
| No pushing. | *No se empuja.* |
| No kicking. | *No se dan patadas.* |
| No pinching. | *No se pellizca.* |
| No spitting. | *No se escupe.* |
| No throwing food. | *La comida no se tira.* |
| No grabbing (things). | *No se arrebata.* |
| No whining. | *No se lloriquea.[2]* |
| Don't tattle. (Don't be a tattletale.) | *No seas soplón.* |
| Always tell the truth. | *Siempre hay que decir la verdad.* |
| Share. | *Hay que compartir.* |
| Include everybody. | *Hay que incluir a todos.* |
| Play with everybody. | *Hay que jugar con todos.* |
| Everyone has to get along. | *Todos tienen que llevarse bien.* |
| Ana, leave the door of your room open. | *Ana, deja abierta la puerta de tu cuarto.* |

And here is a rule that your mother always told you:

| | |
|---|---|
| If you can't say something nice, don't say anything at all. | *Si no puedes decir nada bueno, es mejor no decir nada.* |

---

**GRAMMAR NOTE**

In Spanish to say *one does not hit* (or pinch or anything else), we employ the construction *no se pega* (or *no se pellizca*, etc.) This basically uses the reflexive (pronominal) construction. (You do not need to know the exact rule. Just remembering the above pattern is sufficient.)

---

### Asking permission and waiting

| | |
|---|---|
| If you (all) want to do that, you have to ask permission. | *Si quieres (quieren) hacer eso, tienes (tienen) que pedir permiso.* |

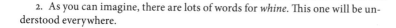

2. As you can imagine, there are lots of words for *whine*. This one will be understood everywhere.

| | |
|---|---|
| Did you (all) ask permission? | *¿Pediste (Pidieron) permiso?* |
| Carla, go ask your mother if it is OK. | *Carla, ve a preguntarle a tu mamá si está bien.* |
| Boys, go ask your uncle if you can go with him. | *Niños, vayan a preguntarle a su tío si pueden ir con él.* |
| Margaret, tell mommy what you want to do. | *Margarita, dile a mami lo que quieres hacer.* |
| Boys, will you tell your father to come here, please? | *Niños, ¿quieren decirle a tu papá que venga, por favor?* |
| Robert, please wait for me. | *Roberto, espérame, por favor.* |
| Girls, wait for us. | *Niñas, espérennos.* |
| Will you (all) wait for us? | *¿Quieres (Quieren) esperarnos?* |
| Will you (all) slow down? | *¿Quieres (Quieren) ir más despacio?* |

## You can't always get what you want

But if you try sometimes, you just might find . . .

| | |
|---|---|
| You can't always get what you want. | *No puedes conseguir siempre lo que quieras.* |
| You can't always have your own way. | *No puedes hacer lo que quieras siempre.* |
| This time we are going to do it her way. | *Esta vez vamos a hacerlo a su manera.* |
| Next time we will do it Olivia's way. | *La próxima vez lo haremos de la forma que quiere Olivia.* |
| Next time we can do it how you want to. | *La próxima vez podemos hacerlo como tú quieras.* |

But then again, maybe not . . . in which case . . .

| | |
|---|---|
| That's life. | *Así es la vida.* |

## Playing calmly

Sometimes you and your kids are in an environment that requires special rules.

| | |
|---|---|
| No running. | *No se corre.* |
| No shouting. | *No se grita.* |

| | |
|---|---|
| The baby is sleeping. | *El bebé está durmiendo.* |
| Mommy is resting. | *Mami está descansando.* |
| You must play quietly. | *Hay que jugar tranquilamente.* |
| You must play silently. | *Hay que jugar en silencio.* |
| Richard, calm down. | *Ricardo, cálmate.* |
| Richard, will you settle down, please? | *Ricardo, ¿quieres calmarte, por favor?* |
| Paul and George, calm down. | *Pablo y Jorge, cálmense.* |
| Paul and George, will you settle down? | *Pablo y Jorge, ¿quieren calmarse?* |
| Eve, do it calmly, please. | *Eva, hazlo con calma, por favor.* |
| Eve and Mary, do it slowly. | *Eva y María, háganlo despacio.* |
| (Take it) Easy! | *¡Suave! (¡Con cuidado!)* |
| Easy with the hamster. | *Suave con el hámster.* |

## Being careful

| | |
|---|---|
| Joseph, please be careful. | *José, ten cuidado, por favor.* |
| Boys, be careful with the statue. | *Niños, tengan cuidado con la estatua.* |
| The vase is fragile. | *El florero es frágil.* |
| The glass breaks easily. | *El vaso se rompe fácilmente.* |
| Those plates break easily. | *Esos platos se rompen fácilmente.* |

## Thank you

| | |
|---|---|
| What do you say? | *¿Qué dices?* |
| Can you (all) tell her thank you? | *¿Puedes (Pueden) darle las gracias?* |

## Taking responsibility and suffering consequences

| | |
|---|---|
| Whose responsibility is it to clean the bathroom? | *¿A quién le toca limpiar el baño?* |
| Robert, it is your responsibility to clean your room. | *Roberto, es tu responsabilidad limpiar tu cuarto.* |
| Monica, do you have something to tell me? | *Mónica, ¿tienes algo que decirme?* |
| Robert, this is not your concern. | *Roberto, esto no es cosa tuya.* |

Sometimes taking responsibility means suffering the consequences.

| | |
|---|---|
| Teresa, because of that you will not be able to go next time. | *Teresa, por eso no vas a poder ir la próxima vez.* |
| For not behaving well, you will have to stay home next time. | *Por no portarte bien, vas a tener que quedarte en casa la próxima vez.* |
| If you (all) cannot listen, there are going to be consequences. | *Si no puedes (pueden) escuchar, entonces va a haber consecuencias.* |

And then there is the infamous *tiempo fuera* (time-out).

| | |
|---|---|
| If you (all) cannot behave yourself, I will give you a time-out. | *Si no puedes (pueden) portarte (portarse) bien, voy a darte (darles) un tiempo fuera.* |
| Do you (all) need a time-out to think about what you did? | *¿Necesitas (Necesitan) un tiempo fuera para pensar en lo que has (han) hecho?* |
| Sit down (you all) in that chair for five minutes. | *Siéntate (Siéntense) en esa silla por cinco minutos.* |
| Clara, if you cannot stop hitting, you are going to have to sit in a chair and play by yourself. | *Clara, si no puedes parar de pegar, entonces vas a tener que sentarte en una silla y jugar sola.* |

### Hurting others and saying sorry

| | |
|---|---|
| Why did you hit her/him? | *¿Por qué le pegaste?* |
| Why did you hurt her/him? | *¿Por qué le hiciste daño?* |
| Why did you hurt her/his feelings? | *¿Por qué le hiciste sentir mal?* |
| Why did you make your little sister cry? | *¿Por qué hiciste llorar a tu hermanita?* |

Of course, it does make a difference if the deed was done on purpose or accidently.

| | |
|---|---|
| Adrian, did you do it on purpose? | *Adrián, ¿lo hiciste a propósito?* |
| You did it by accident? | *¿Lo hiciste sin querer?* |
| I see. It was an accident. | *Ya veo. Fue un accidente.* |

But if it was on purpose:

| | |
|---|---|
| That was not very nice. | *Eso no fue muy simpático.* |
| That wasn't very kind. | *Eso no fue muy amable.* |
| Tell him you are sorry. | *Dile que lo sientes.* |
| Give your sister a kiss. | *Dale un beso a tu hermana.* |
| Give your little brother a hug. | *Dale un abrazo a tu hermanito.* |

## HELPING OUT

**KEY VOCABULARY:**

broom, *la escoba*
bucket, *el cubo*
detergent, *la detergente*
dishwasher, *el lavaplatos*
dryer, *la secadora*
mop, *la fregona*
rag, *el trapo*
soap, *el jabón*
sponge, *la esponja*
vacuum cleaner, *la aspiradora*
washing machine, *la lavadora*

to clean your room, *limpiar tu cuarto*
to clear the table, *recoger la mesa*
to cut the grass, *cortar el césped*

to dry (the dishes), *secar (los platos)*
to dust, *quitar el polvo*
to mop, *pasar la fregona*
to pick up, *recoger*
to rake the leaves, *recoger las hojas*
to rake the yard, *rastrillar el césped*
to rinse, *enjuagar*
to set the table, *poner la mesa*
to do the shopping, *hacer las compras*
to sweep, *barrer*
to take out the garbage, *sacar la basura*
to vacuum, *pasar la aspiradora*
to wash (clothes), *lavar (la ropa)*
to wash the car, *lavar el carro*[3]
to wash the dishes, *lavar los platos*
to wash the windows, *lavar las ventanas*

### Picking up and other things to do around the house

| | |
|---|---|
| David, let's make your bed. | *David, vamos a hacer tu cama.* |
| David, did you make your bed? | *David, ¿hiciste tu cama?* |
| Girls, will you make your beds? | *Niñas, ¿quieren hacer sus camas?* |
| Did you make your beds? | *¿Hicieron sus camas?* |
| Ellen, did you pick up your room? | *Elena, ¿recogiste tu cuarto?* |
| Boys, did you clean your room? | *Niños, ¿limpiaron su cuarto?* |
| Carlos, did you do your chores today? | *Carlos, ¿hiciste tus quehaceres hoy?* |
| Here is your allowance. | *Aquí tienes tu domingo.*[4] |

---

3. There is a wide variation in the translation for *car* throughout the Spanish-speaking world. In this text we use *carro*, common in many parts of Mexico, Central America, and northern South America. "*Coche*" is also common. "*Automóvil*," though a bit formal for most situations, is universally understood.

4. In Latin America your allowance is *el domingo* even if you do not receive it on Sunday. In Spain you might say *el pago semanal*.

## TALKING ON THE TELEPHONE

**KEY VOCABULARY:**

telephone, *el teléfono*          to talk, *hablar*
cell phone, *el celular*          to dial, *marcar*
number, *el número*               to hang up, *colgar*
to answer, *contestar*

From the time that they can talk, kids want to use the phone. At some point, they figure out how to do it.

| | |
|---|---|
| You may answer the telephone. | *Puedes contestar el teléfono.* |
| Say hello and tell them who you are. | *Dile hola y dile quién eres.* |
| Say, "Hello, I'm Paul. Who is speaking, please?" | *Dile, "Hola, soy Pablo. ¿Quién habla, por favor?"* |
| Who is it, please? | *¿Quién es, por favor?* |
| I will dial the number and then you can talk. | *Voy a marcar el número y después puedes hablar.* |

Sometimes small kids just stand there, transfixed by the experience, while the person on the other end of the line is saying, "Johnny? Are you there, Johnny? . . ."

| | |
|---|---|
| John, you have to say something. | *Juan, tienes que decir algo.* |
| John, you have to speak loudly. | *Juan, tienes que hablar fuerte.* |
| Tell her goodbye and give me the phone, please. | *Dile adiós y dame el teléfono, por favor.* |
| Hang up the telephone, please. | *Cuelga el teléfono, por favor.* |

And then there are the times when *you* are on the telephone.

| | |
|---|---|
| I am talking on the telephone. | *Estoy hablando por teléfono.* |
| You will have to wait. | *Tienes que esperar.* |
| You will have to wait until I am done. | *Tienes que esperar a que termine.* |

# PLAY, PRESCHOOL, AND SCHOOL

## JUST PLAYING

ball, *una pelota*
    baseball, *la pelota de béisbol*
    larger, inflated ball, *el balón*
bicycle, *la bicicleta*
board game, *el juego de mesa*
    board, *la tabla*
    dice, *los dados*
    game piece, *la pieza*
doll, *la muñeca*
game, *el juego*
playing cards, *las cartas*
    deck, *la baraja*
puzzle, *el rompecabezas*

skates, *los patines*
    ice skates, *los patines de hielo*
    roller skates, *los patines de ruedas*
sled, *el trineo*
toy, *el juguete*
toy train, *el tren de juguete*

to go for a walk, *ir de paseo*
to joke, *bromear*
to jump, *saltar*
to play (a game), *jugar*
to play (a musical instrument), *tocar*

---

### Let's play

"Let's do something" is most readily translated as *Vamos a* plus the infinitive of what you want to do.

Let's play.
What are we going to play?

*Vamos a jugar.*
*¿A qué vamos a jugar?*

| | |
|---|---|
| I have an idea. | *Tengo una idea.* |
| Something has occurred to me. | *Se me ocurrió algo.* |
| Do you (all) want to read a book? | *¿Quieres (Quieren) leer un libro?* |
| Let's dance. | *Vamos a bailar.* |
| Do you (all) like to swim? | *¿Te (les) gusta nadar?* |
| Let's go swimming. | *Vamos a nadar.* |
| Javier is listening to music. | *Javier está escuchando la música.* |
| Let's play the piano. | *Vamos a tocar el piano.* |
| We should take the dog for a walk. | *Debemos pasear al perro.* |
| Let's do a project. | *Vamos a hacer un proyecto.* |
| It's a nice day to ride bikes. | *Es un buen día para montar en bicicleta (en bici).* |
| Let's go skating. | *Vamos a patinar.* |
| We can go ice-skating tomorrow. | *Podemos patinar sobre hielo mañana.* |
| Let's do a puzzle. | *Vamos a hacer un rompecabezas.* |

For a couple of activities, there is a slightly different construction:

| | |
|---|---|
| Why don't we go for a walk? | *¿Por qué no vamos de paseo?* |
| Let's go shopping. | *Vamos de compras.* |
| Do you (all) want to go sledding? | *¿Quieres (Quieren) ir en trineo?* |
| James, do you want to play with blocks? | *Jaime, ¿quieres jugar con bloques?* |
| James and Martha, do you want to jump rope? | *Jaime y Marta, ¿quieren saltar la cuerda (saltar la reata)?* |
| Christine and Paul, do you want to play with the toy trains? | *Cristina y Pablo, ¿quieren jugar con los trenes de juguete?* |
| Christine, do you want to play with your dolls? | *Cristina, ¿quieres jugar con tus muñecas?* |

For variety, you can use "*Te gustaría . . .*" (for one kid) and "*Les gustaría . . .*" (for more than one kid). These translate, "Would you like to . . . ?"

| | |
|---|---|
| Anne, would you like to draw outside with chalk? | *Ana, ¿te gustaría dibujar afuera con la tiza?* |
| Anne and Louis, would you like to watch a movie? | *Ana y Luis, ¿les gustaría ver una película?* |
| Louis, would you like to play cards? | *Luis, ¿te gustaría jugar a las cartas?* |

Of course, your kids may have already decided on their own what they are going to do. In this case you may want to ask them:

| | |
|---|---|
| Angela, what are you doing? | *Ángela, ¿qué haces?* |
| Angela and Edward, what are you doing? | *Ángela y Eduardo, ¿qué hacen?* |
| Angela, what are you going to do? | *Ángela, ¿qué vas a hacer?* |
| Kids, what are you going to do? | *Niños, ¿qué van a hacer?* |
| Angela, what are you playing? | *Ángela, ¿a qué juegas?* |
| Angela and Edward, what are you playing? | *Ángela y Eduardo, ¿a qué juegan?* |

## Let's pretend

Kids love to play pretend, and they love to include you in their play. The problem for English speakers (and this vexed us for quite some time) is that you cannot use the Spanish verb *pretender* in these situations. In Spanish there is no way to say *Let's play pretend* or *Let's play make-believe* without saying what, in particular, you are going to make believe about. What do you use? One possibility, and probably the easiest, is to use *hacer de cuenta que* . . . Another common form is *jugar a que* . . . (to play that . . .)

| | |
|---|---|
| Let's play pretend. | *Vamos a jugar.* |
| I am going to pretend that I am the king. | *Voy a hacer de cuenta que soy el rey.* |
| Tom, pretend that you are a dog and that John is your puppy. | *Tom, haz de cuenta que eres un perro y que Juan es tu cachorro.* |
| Anthony, let's play that you are a cat and that Henry is your kitten. | *Antonio, vamos a jugar a que tú eres un gato y que Enrique es tu gatito.* |
| Isabel and Olivia, pretend that you are students and that I am your teacher. | *Isabel y Olivia, hagan de cuenta que ustedes son alumnas y que yo soy su maestro.* |
| Thomas, let's play that you are the teacher and that this room is your school. | *Tomás, vamos a jugar a que eres el maestro y que este cuarto es tu escuela.* |

Once you are ensconced in the game, you can talk as if pretend were real. The great thing about young children is that the line between pretend and real is really no line at all.

| | |
|---|---|
| Let's be a family of cats. | *Vamos a ser una familia de gatos.* |
| Saraí, you can be the mother and Thomas can be the father. | *Saraí, puedes ser la mamá y Tomás puede ser el papá.* |
| Kids, you can be animals of the forest. | *Niños, pueden ser animales del bosque.* |

Sometimes you may have to be the arbiter in the world of pretend.

| | |
|---|---|
| Isabel, let Thomas be the puppy. | *Isabel, deja que Tomás sea el cachorro.* |
| Isabel, let Eva be the fairy. | *Isabel, deja que Eva sea el hada.* |
| Isabel y Thomas, let your little sister be what she wants. | *Isabel y Tomás, dejen que su hermanita sea lo que quiera.* |
| Isabel, let everyone be what they want. | *Isabel, deja que todos sean lo que quieran.* |

To distinguish between the real world and the pretend world, you can use *de verdad* and *de juguete.*

| | |
|---|---|
| It isn't a real dog. | *No es un perro de verdad.* |
| It's a toy dog. | *Es un perro de juguete.* |
| You can't really eat that. | *No puedes comer eso de verdad.* |
| I am not really sleeping. | *No estoy durmiendo de verdad.* |
| I am just faking. | *Sólo estoy fingiendo.* |
| You can pretend to eat it. | *Puedes hacer de cuenta que lo comes.* |

## Kidding around

To joke is *bromear.* A joke, as in a funny story, is *un chiste.* A joke, as in a prank, is *una broma.*

| | |
|---|---|
| I was just joking. | *Sólo estaba bromeando.* |
| I did it as a joke. | *Lo hice en broma.* |
| It was a practical joke. | *Fue una broma pesada.* |
| I am going to tell you all a joke. | *Voy a contarles un chiste.* |
| Alexandra is going to tell us a joke. | *Alejandra va a contarnos un chiste.* |

Sometimes your kids may do something that they think is funny, but you may fail to see the humor in it and may wish to express this.

| | |
|---|---|
| I don't think that is so funny. | *No le veo la gracia.* |

## Playing ball

| | |
|---|---|
| Alice, do you want to play ball? | *Alicia, ¿quieres jugar a la pelota?* |
| Kids, do you want to play soccer? | *Niños, ¿quieren jugar al fútbol?* |
| Richard, do you want to play catch? | *Ricardo, ¿quieres jugar a atrapar la pelota?* |
| Throw me the ball. | *Tírame la pelota.* |
| Kick the ball. | *Patea la pelota. (Dale una patada a la pelota).* |
| Catch the ball. | *Atrapa la pelota.* |
| Throw the ball to your brother. | *Lánzale la pelota a tu hermano.* |
| Girls, do you want to play basketball? | *Niñas, quieren jugar al básquetbol (baloncesto)?* |
| Ana, shoot the ball in the basket. | *Ana, lanza el balón a la canasta.* |
| I won. | *Gané.* |
| You (all) won. | *Ganaste (Ganaron).* |
| We won. | *Ganamos.* |
| I lost. | *Perdí.* |
| Javier and Lucia lost. | *Javier y Lucía perdieron.* |
| Lucia and I lost again. | *Lucía y yo perdimos otra vez.* |

## Tag, hide-and-seek, house, hopscotch, etc.

| | |
|---|---|
| Let's play tag. | *Vamos a jugar a encantados.* |
| Margaret, you are "It." | *Margarita, te toca a ti buscar.* |
| Do you (all) want to play house? | *¿Quieres (quieren) jugar a la casita?* |
| Let's play dress-up. | *Vamos a jugar a disfrazarnos.* |
| I want to dress up as a cowboy. | *Quiero disfrazarme de vaquero.* |
| Let's play monster. | *Vamos a jugar al monstruo.* |
| We're going to play hopscotch. | *Vamos a jugar a la rayuela.* |
| Anne and Louis, would you like to play hide-and-seek? | *Ana y Luis, ¿les gustaría jugar a las escondidas (al escondite)?* |
| I'm going to hide. You two can hide next time. | *Me voy a esconder. Ustedes dos se pueden esconder la próxima vez.* |

## Fun, funny, and a little strange

To be fun is to be *divertido*. To be funny, in the sense that makes you laugh, is *chistoso* or *gracioso*. To be strange or odd is to be *raro*.

| | |
|---|---|
| That's really fun. | *Eso es muy divertido.* |
| Margarite is really funny. | *Margarita es muy chistosa.* |
| This movie is a bit strange. | *Esta película es un poco rara.* |

## The playground

Kids spend a lot of time on the playground and, consequently, so do you.

| | |
|---|---|
| Let's go to the new playground. | *Vamos al nuevo patio de recreo.* |
| What is there in that playground? | *¿Qué hay en aquel patio de recreo?* |
| There are swings and slides. | *Hay columpios y resbaladillas (toboganes).* |
| There is a jungle gym with bars, bridges, and tunnels. | *Hay juegos para trepar con barras, puentes y túneles.* |
| Also, there is a sandbox and a fountain. | *También hay una caja de arena y una fuente.* |
| Theresa, do you want to swing? | *Teresa, ¿quieres columpiarte?* |
| Kids, do you want to swing? | *Niños, ¿quieren columpiarse?* |
| Where are the swings? | *¿Dónde están los columpios?* |
| Do you want me to push you? | *¿Quieres que te empuje?* |
| Tanya, do you want to go higher? | *Tania, ¿quieres ir más alto?* |
| Tanya, can you do it by yourself? | *Tania, ¿puedes hacerlo sola?* |
| Jude, do you know how to swing yourself? | *Judas, ¿sabes empujarte solo?* |
| Don't (you all) go too high. | *No vayas (vayan) muy alto.* |
| Do you (all) want to slide? | *¿Quieres (quieren) resbalarte (resbalarse)?* |
| Did you climb on the jungle gym? | *¿Trepaste por los juegos?* |
| Do you (all) want to play in the sand box? | *¿Quieres (Quieren) jugar en la caja de arena?* |
| Do you (all) need a shovel? | *¿Necesitas (Necesitan) una pala?* |
| Don't (you all) throw sand. | *No tires (tiren) arena.* |
| Please keep the sand in the box. | *Deja (Dejen) la arena en la caja, por favor.* |

# DRAWING, COLORING, CUTTING, AND PASTING

**KEY VOCABULARY:**

card, *la tarjeta*
colored paper, *el papel de color*
crayon, *el crayón, la crayola*
glue, *el pegamento*
paintbrush, *el pincel*
painting, *un cuadro*
paper, *el papel*
scissors, *las tijeras*
sheet of paper, *la hoja de papel*
watercolors, *las acuarelas*

to color, *colorear*
to cut out, *recortar*
to draw, *dibujar*
to glue, *pegar*
to show, *enseñar, mostrar*
to trace, *trazar*

## Doing art

Our kids spend so much time drawing and coloring and cutting and pasting and, in general, doing little projects, that we find that a great deal of parent-child interaction goes on around these activities. Indeed, this is a great opportunity to talk to your kids in Spanish.

## Let's do art!

| | |
|---|---|
| Let's color. | *Vamos a colorear.* |
| Let's draw. | *Vamos a dibujar.* |
| Let's do a project. | *Vamos a hacer un proyecto.* |
| Bobby, do you want to color? | *Bobby, ¿quieres colorear?* |
| Saraí and Maya, do you want to draw? | *Saraí y Maya, ¿quieren dibujar?* |
| Ricky, do you want to paint? | *Riki, ¿quieres pintar?* |
| Let's make a birthday card for your grandma. | *Vamos a hacer una tarjeta de cumpleaños para tu abuelita.* |
| Let's make a drawing for mommy's office. | *Vamos a hacer un dibujo para la oficina de mami.* |
| Let's do a painting for daddy. | *Vamos a hacer un cuadro para papi.* |

## Getting materials together

| | |
|---|---|
| Lisa, do you want some paper? | *Lisa, ¿quieres papel?* |
| Boys, do you want some crayons? | *Niños, ¿quieren crayones (crayolas)?* |
| Mark, do you want some watercolors? | *Mark, ¿quieres acuarelas?* |
| Bobby, do you need some water? | *Bobby, ¿necesitas agua?* |
| Bobby and Martha, do you need paintbrushes? | *Bobby y Marta, ¿necesitan pinceles?* |
| Ricky, do you need scissors? | *Riki, ¿necesitas tijeras?* |
| Monica and Maya, do you need glue? | *Mónica y Maya, ¿necesitan pegamento?* |
| Pass me the scissors, please. | *Pásame las tijeras, por favor.* |
| Pass me the glue, please. | *Pásame el pegamento, por favor.* |

## Getting to work

| | |
|---|---|
| Are you (all) going to paint? | *¿Vas (van) a pintar?* |
| Louis, are you going to cut that paper? | *Luis, ¿vas a cortar ese papel?* |
| Angela, are you going to make shapes with that colored paper? | *Ángela, ¿vas a hacer figuras con ese papel de color?* |
| Steven, try not to tear that paper. | *Esteban, trata de no romper ese papel.* |
| Richard, are you going to glue it? | *Ricardo, ¿vas a pegarlo?* |

## Colors

Some colors change according to the number and gender of the word being described. Some vary with number but not gender. Some do not vary at all. Thus you have a *pájaro rojo* (red bird) and *casas rojas* (red houses). On the other hand, you have *pájaro rosa* and *casas rosa*.[1] For a list of colors and for an explanation of how they are used, please see "Colors" in our grammar section, "Grammar Enough to Get You Started."

---

1. Sometimes you hear *casas rosas*, but you would never hear *pájaros rosos*.

## Tell me about it

When talking to your child about his or her drawing, you probably are going to want to express approval and to discuss the picture. The typical way to say that you like something is *Me gusta* plus the thing that you like. If you like more than one thing, you would say *Me gustan*.

| | |
|---|---|
| Olivia, I like your drawing. | *Olivia, me gusta tu dibujo.* |
| I like it a lot. | *Me gusta mucho.* |
| I like the colors. | *Me gustan los colores.* |
| I like the tree. | *Me gusta el árbol.* |
| It is very pretty. | *Es muy bonito.* |
| I like the moon. | *Me gusta la luna.* |
| The moon is very pretty. | *La luna es muy bonita.* |

Kids love talking about and explaining their art projects. All you need to do is to ask a few questions.

| | |
|---|---|
| What is this? | *¿Qué es esto?* |
| What is that? | *¿Qué es eso?* |
| What is it made out of? | *¿De qué es?* |
| | *¿De qué está hecho?* |
| It is papier-mâché. | *Es de cartón piedra.* |
| It is made out of wood and wire. | *Está hecho de madera y alambre.* |
| What is this circle? | *¿Qué es este círculo?* |
| What is that square? | *¿Qué es ese cuadrado?* |
| What is that rectangle? | *¿Qué es ese rectángulo?* |
| What is that diamond? | *¿Qué es ese rombo?* |
| Is it a house? | *¿Es una casa?* |
| Oh, it is a bird. | *Ah, es un pájaro.* |
| Is it the sun? | *¿Es el sol?* |
| Oh, it is the moon. | *Ah, es la luna.* |
| It's a tree. | *Es un árbol.* |
| It's grass. | *Es hierba.* |
| Is it a cow? | *¿Es una vaca?* |
| Oh, it's a horse. | *Ah, es un caballo.* |
| Who is that person? | *¿Quién es esa persona?* |
| Who is this man? | *¿Quién es este hombre?* |
| Who is that woman? | *¿Quién es esa mujer?* |

| Who is that boy? Who is that child? | ¿Quién es ese niño? |
| Who is this girl? | ¿Quién es esta niña? |
| Who is that baby? | ¿Quién es ese bebé? |
| Is it Victoria? | ¿Es Victoria? |
| Oh, it is your little sister. | Ah, es tu hermanita. |

## Cleanup time

| It's time to clean up. | Es hora de recoger. |
| It's time to put everything away. | Es hora de guardarlo todo. |

A nice way to ask kids to do things is to begin the phrase with *Quieres* or *Quieren* (depending on how many kids you are talking to) which just means "Will you . . .?" Attaching *por favor* (please) makes it even nicer.

| Ronny, will you please pick up? | Roni, ¿quieres recoger, por favor? |
| Kids, will you please put everything away? | Niños, ¿quieren guardarlo todo, por favor? |
| Mary, will you pick up the paper? | María, ¿quieres recoger el papel? |
| Lucas and Claire, will you put away the crayons? | Lucas y Clara, ¿quieren guardar las crayolas? |

## SCHOOL AND EXTRACURRICULARS

The average American kid spends a lot of time in school, preschool, and child care. This is fertile ground for conversation. Again, you have to ask the right questions.

**KEY VOCABULARY:**

baseball (the game), *el béisbol*
basketball (the game), *el básquetbol,*
   *el baloncesto*
book, *el libro*
bus, *el autobús, el bus*
class, *la clase*
   science class, *la clase de ciencias*
   art class, *la clase de arte*
   history class, *la clase de historia*
   computer class, *la clase de*
      *computación*
   music class, *la clase de música*
   dance class, *la clase de baile*
   swimming class, *la clase de*
      *natación*
   acting class, *la clase de actuación*

football (the game), *el fútbol*
   *americano*
gym, *el gimnasio*
library, *la biblioteca*
playground, *el patio de recreo*
practice, rehearsal, *la práctica, el ensayo*
project, *el proyecto*
   science project, *el proyecto de*
      *ciencias*
school, *la escuela, el colegio (el cole)*
soccer, *el fútbol*
teacher, *el maestro, la maestra*

to go to class, *asistir, ir a clase*
to study, *estudiar*

### What did you do at school today?

Monica, what did you do today at school? — *Mónica, ¿qué hiciste hoy en la escuela?*

Girls, what did you all do today at your art class? — *Niñas, ¿qué hicieron hoy en su clase de arte?*

If your kids are like ours, the response to the foregoing two questions is invariably, "Nada." I tend to have more luck with the following:

Who can tell me one thing that they did at school today? — *¿Quién puede decirme una cosa que hizo en la escuela hoy?*

Noah, can you tell me one thing that you did at school today? — *Noé, ¿puedes decirme una cosa que hiciste en la escuela hoy?*

| | |
|---|---|
| Did you (all) sing? | ¿Cantaste? (¿Cantaron?) |
| Did you (all) read a book? | ¿Leíste (Leyeron) un libro? |
| Did your teacher read you all a story? | ¿Su maestra les leyó un cuento? |
| Do you all have any new books at school? | ¿Tienen algunos libros nuevos en la escuela? |

## Learning to observe

| | |
|---|---|
| Jude, what was your teacher wearing today? | Judas, ¿qué llevaba tu maestra hoy? |
| Which friends were at school today? | ¿Qué amigos estaban en la escuela hoy? |
| Whom did you (all) play with today? | ¿Con quién jugaste (jugaron) hoy? |

## Don't know much about history . . .

| | |
|---|---|
| What did you (all) talk about today in school? | ¿De qué hablaste (hablaron) hoy en la escuela? |
| Did you (all) talk about the days of the week or the seasons of the year? | ¿Hablaste (Hablaron) de los días de la semana o de las estaciones del año? |
| Did you (all) look at a map today in school? | ¿Miraste (Miraron) un mapa hoy en la escuela? |
| Did you (all) talk about a country today? | ¿Hablaste (Hablaron) acerca de un país hoy? |
| Did you (all) talk about people in other places of the world today? | ¿Hablaste (Hablaron) de personas de otros lugares del mundo hoy? |
| Did you (all) do a science project? | ¿Hiciste (Hicieron) un proyecto de ciencias? |
| What did you (all) study in science today? | ¿Qué estudiaste (estudiaron) en la clase de ciencias hoy? |
| Did you (all) do something with numbers today? | ¿Hiciste (Hicieron) algo con números hoy? |
| Did you (all) do counting today? | ¿Contaste (Contaron) con números hoy? |
| Did you (all) do addition and subtraction today? | ¿Hiciste (Hicieron) sumas y restas hoy? |

## Gym class, art class, library, and more

| | |
|---|---|
| Did you (all) go to the library today? | ¿Fuiste (Fueron) a la biblioteca hoy? |
| Did you (all) check out any new books? | ¿Sacaste (sacaron) algunos libros nuevos? |
| Did you (all) go to the gym today? | ¿Fuiste (Fueron) al gimnasio hoy? |
| Did you (all) go to gym class today? | ¿Fuiste (Fueron) a la clase de educación física[2] hoy? |
| Did you (all) have art class? | ¿Tuviste (Tuvieron) la clase de arte hoy? |
| What did you (all) do in your art class? | ¿Qué hiciste (hicieron) en la clase de arte? |
| Did you (all) draw something? | ¿Dibujaste (Dibujaron) algo? |
| What did you (all) paint? | ¿Qué pintaste (pintaron)? |
| Did you (all) bring your drawing home? | ¿Trajiste (Trajeron) el dibujo a casa? |
| Did you (all) go to computer class? | ¿Fuiste (Fueron) a la clase de computación? |
| Did you (all) have fun today? | ¿Te divertiste (Se divirtieron) hoy? |
| Did you (all) learn something new today? | ¿Aprendiste (Aprendieron) algo nuevo hoy? |
| What did you (all) learn today? | ¿Qué aprendiste (aprendieron) hoy? |
| Can you (all) tell me something new that you (all) learned today? | ¿Puedes (Pueden) decirme una cosa nueva que aprendiste (aprendieron) hoy? |
| What friends did you (all) see today? | ¿A qué amigos viste (vieron) hoy? |
| With which friends did you (all) play today? | ¿Con qué amigos jugaste (jugaron) hoy? |
| What did you (all) play? | ¿A qué jugaste (jugaron)? |
| What are you (all) going to do tomorrow at school? | ¿Qué vas (van) a hacer mañana en la escuela? |

## School lunch

| | |
|---|---|
| Alexandra, you bought your lunch today, right? | Alejandra, compraste el almuerzo hoy, ¿verdad? |
| What did you buy for lunch? | ¿Qué compraste para almorzar? |
| Did you like it? | ¿Te gustó? |

---

2. A gymnastics class would be *una clase de gimnasia.*

| | |
|---|---|
| What did you like? What didn't you like? | ¿Qué te gustó? ¿Qué no te gustó? |
| Did you try everything? Did you eat everything? | ¿Probaste todo? ¿Comiste todo? |
| It's OK. You don't have to like everything. | Está bien. No importa que no te guste todo. |
| You should try everything to see if you like it. | Deberías probar todo para ver si te gusta. |
| What was the dessert? | ¿Cuál fue el postre? |
| With whom did you eat? | ¿Con quién comiste? |
| What did she have for lunch? | ¿Qué almorzó ella? |

## Recess

| | |
|---|---|
| Did you (all) go outside today? | ¿Saliste (Salieron) afuera hoy? |
| Adrian, did you go to the school playground? | Adrián, ¿fuiste al patio de recreo? |
| Did you swing? | ¿Te columpiaste? |
| Did you slide? | ¿Te tiraste por la resbaladilla (el tobogán)? |
| Did you climb on the jungle gym? | ¿Te subiste a los juegos? |

## How was the field trip?

| | |
|---|---|
| Did you all go on a field trip today? | ¿Fueron en una excursión hoy? |
| Where did you all go? | ¿Adónde fueron? |
| Did you all go to the museum? | ¿Fueron al museo? |
| And what did you all do there? | ¿Y qué hicieron por allí? |
| What did you (all) see there? | ¿Qué viste (vieron) allí? |
| Who all went? | ¿Quiénes fueron? |
| Did the whole class go? | ¿Fue toda la clase? |
| Did some adults go too? | ¿Fueron también algunos adultos? |
| Did any parents go? | ¿Fueron algunos papás? |
| How did you all go, walking or by bus? | ¿Cómo fueron, caminando o en autobús?[3] |
| Did you have a partner? | ¿Tuviste a un compañero? |
| Where did you all eat lunch? | ¿Dónde almorzaron? |

---

3. In many parts of Mexico *camión* is used for bus.

## Homework and other stuff sent home

Teachers often send things home with kids, including homework, notes from the teacher, work they did in school, report cards, and announcements of events.

| | |
|---|---|
| Did your teacher give you anything to bring home? | *¿Te dio algo tu maestra para traer a casa?* |
| What did your teacher give you? | *¿Qué te dio tu maestra?* |
| Did your teacher give you any homework? | *¿Te dio tu maestra tarea?* |
| Do you have something to prepare for tomorrow? | *¿Tienes que preparar algo para mañana?* |
| Do you need help with your homework? | *¿Necesitas ayuda con tu tarea?* |

## Soccer practice and ballet classes

These days, kids have lots of activities. It seems as if you are always running to this activity or that one. Here are a few:

| | |
|---|---|
| Let's go to your swimming class. | *Vamos a la clase de natación.* |
| Let's go to your art class. | *Vamos a la clase de arte.* |
| It's time to go to your dance class. | *Es hora de ir a la clase de baile.* |
| Your acting class begins soon. | *La clase de actuación empieza pronto.* |
| Let's go to the rehearsal. | *Vamos al ensayo.* |
| Your music class ends at five. | *La clase de música termina a las cinco.* |
| You have piano class on Wednesday. | *Tienes la clase de piano los miércoles.* |
| You have violin class in the morning. | *Tienes la clase de violín por la mañana.* |
| Your flute class was canceled today. | *La clase de flauta fue cancelada hoy.* |
| Get ready for soccer practice. | *Prepárate para la práctica de fútbol.* |

# TELEVISION, MOVIES, AND MUSIC

**KEY VOCABULARY:**

channel, *el canal*
movie theater, cinema, *el cine*
drum, *el tambor*
flute, *la flauta*
guitar, *la guitarra*
instrument, *el instrumento*
movie, *la película*
piano, *el piano*

popcorn, *las palomitas*
program, *el programa*
television, *la televisión*
television set, *el televisor*

to turn off, *apagar*
to turn on, *encender*

## Television and Movies

Again, television, if not overused, can be a wonderful way of reinforcing language.

| | |
|---|---|
| Do you (all) want to go to the movies? | *¿Quieres (Quieren) ir al cine?* |
| Marcos, do you want to watch television? | *Marcos, ¿quieres ver la televisión?* |
| Girls, do you want to watch TV? | *Niñas, ¿quieren ver la tele?* |
| Paula, do you want to watch a movie? | *Paula, ¿quieres ver una película? (una peli)* |
| What movie do you want? | *¿Qué película quieres?* |
| Adrian and Alfredo, what program do you want? | *Adrián y Alfredo, ¿qué programa quieren?* |
| You can watch for a half hour. | *Pueden verla por media hora.* |
| You can watch until seven-thirty. | *Pueden verla hasta las siete y media.* |
| Would you like to eat some popcorn? | *¿Les gustaría comer palomitas?* |
| Does anyone have the remote? | *¿Tiene alguien el control remoto?* |
| Thomas, will you change the channel please? | *Tomás, ¿quieres cambiar el canal, por favor?* |
| Put it on channel two, please. | *Pon el canal dos, por favor.* |
| You can put the video in the video deck. | *Puedes meter el video en la video.[4]* |

---

4. *La video* is short for *la videocasetera*. *El video* is the videotape.

| | |
|---|---|
| Can you eject the tape? | *¿Puedes sacar el video?* |
| I am going to rewind the tape. | *Voy a rebobinar el video.* |
| Where is the *Living Forest* DVD?[5] | *¿Dónde está el DVD de* El bosque animado? |
| | |
| It's in the DVD player. | *Está en el DVD.* |
| Put it in its case, please. | *Ponlo en su caja, por favor.* |
| Ok, kids, do you want to see *Charlie and the Chocolate Factory?* | *Bien, niños, ¿quieren ver* Charlie y la fábrica de chocolate? |
| Put in the disk, Laura. | *Mete el DVD, Laura.* |
| Let's change the language to Spanish. | *Vamos a cambiar el idioma al español.* |
| Michael, select "menu," then select "languages" and then "Spanish." | *Miguel, selecciona "menú," luego selecciona "lenguas" y entonces "español."* |
| | |
| We can rent another movie next weekend. | *Podemos alquilar otra peli el fin de semana que viene.* |
| Lisa, you are in the way. | *Lisa, estás estorbando.* |
| Lisa, you are not letting us see. | *Lisa, no nos dejas ver.*[6] |
| Move, please. | *Muévete, por favor.* |
| Can you all move a bit to the right? (to the left) | *¿Pueden moverse todos un poco a la derecha? (a la izquierda)?* |
| We cannot hear. | *No podemos oír.* |
| We have to be quiet. | *Tenemos que guardar silencio.* |
| Daniela, will you turn up (turn down) the volume, please? | *Daniela, ¿quieres subir (bajar) el volumen, por favor?* |
| Turn off the TV, please. | *Apaga la tele, por favor.* |

## Making music

Kids love to sing, dance, and make music.

| | |
|---|---|
| Let's make music. | *Vamos a hacer música.* |
| Let's choose instruments. | *Vamos a escoger instrumentos.* |
| Do you all want to play the drums? | *¿Quieren todos tocar el tambor?* |
| Who wants the tambourine? | *¿Quién quiere la pandereta?* |
| Who wants to sing? | *¿Quién quiere cantar?* |

---

5. DVD is just *DVD* (pronounced in Spanish *they-ooveh-they*) and is used to refer to both the disk and the machine.

6. Or you might say, "La carne de burro no es transparente," a good-natured jab.

| | |
|---|---|
| Who wants to dance? | *¿Quién quiere bailar?* |
| Listen (you all) to the rhythm. | *Escucha (Escuchen) el ritmo.* |
| Let's march to the beat of the music. | *Vamos a marchar al compás de la música.* |

As for recorded music:

| | |
|---|---|
| Let's put on some music. | *Vamos a poner un poco de música.* |
| What cassette tape do you (all) want? | *¿Qué cinta quieres (quieren)?* |
| What CD do you (all) want? | *¿Qué CD quieres (quieren)?* |
| Let's put the CD on track 5. | *Vamos a poner el CD en la pista cinco.* |
| What record do you (all) want? | *¿Qué disco quieres (quieren)?* |
| I am going to rewind the cassette. | *Voy a rebobinar la cinta.* |
| Put the tape in the tape player, please. | *Pon la cinta en la grabadora, por favor.* |
| I am going to record a tape. | *Voy a grabar una cinta.* |
| Where is the tape recorder? | *¿Dónde está la grabadora?* |

# COMPUTERS AND THE INTERNET

### KEY VOCABULARY (COMPUTERS):

address (e-mail, web), *la dirección (de correo electrónico, de web)*

backup, *la copia de seguridad*

battery, *la pila*

bookmark, *el marcapáginas*

browser, *el navegador*

bulletin board, *el tablón de anuncios*

button, *el botón*

cable, *el cable*

cartridge, *el cartucho*

CD-ROM, *el CD-ROM*

chat, *el chateo*

chat room, *la sala de charla*

compact disc, *el disco compacto*

compatible, *compatible*

computer, *la computadora*

cursor, *el cursor*

cybercafé, *el cibercafé*

default, *la opción por defecto*

disk (backup), *el disco (de seguridad)*

e-mail, *el correo electrónico*

empty, *vacío*

file, *el archivo*

folder, *la carpeta*

GB (Gigabyte), *el GB (gigabyte)*

graphics, *los gráficos*

hacker, *el pirata*

hard disk, *el disco duro*

home page, *la página inicial*

icon, *el icono*

IM (instant messaging), *la mensajería instantánea*

image, *la imagen*

ink, *la tinta*

interactive, *interactivo*

Internet, *el Internet*

Internet Explorer, *el Explorador Internet*

junk mail, *el correo basura*

keyboard, *el teclado*

keyword, *la palabra clave*

laptop, *la computadora portátil*

link, *el enlace*

MB (megabyte), *el MB (megabyte)*

memory, *la memoria*

menu, *el menú*

monitor, *el monitor*

mouse, *el ratón*

network, *la red*

off-line, *desconectado, fuera de línea*

online, *conectado, en línea*

page, *la página*

password, *la contraseña*

power, *la energía, la corriente*

printer, *la impresora*

scanner, *el escáner*

screen, *la pantalla*

server, *el servidor*

site, *el sitio*

software, *el programa, el software*

system, *el sistema*

user name, *el nombre de usuario*

virus, *el virus*

volume, *el volumen*

web, *el web*

web page, *la página web*

webcam, *la cámara web*

website, *el sitio web*

to back up, *hacer una copia de seguridad*

to boot up, *arrancar*

to chat, *charlar*

to click, *hacer clic*

to connect, *conectar*

to delete, *borrar*

to double click, *hacer doble clic*

to download, *descargar, bajarse*

to install, *instalar*

to navigate (to), *navegar*

to print, *imprimir*

to reboot, *arrancar de nuevo*

to recover, *recuperar*

to right-click (left-click), *darle al botón derecho (izquierdo) del ratón*

to save, *guardar*

to search, *buscar*

to select, choose, *escoger, seleccionar*

to upgrade, *actualizar*

to upload, *cargar, subirse*

## Computers

Computers can be great language-learning tools. More and more programs are being written in Spanish and for Spanish. A lot of computer vocabulary is in English.

| | |
|---|---|
| Kids, do you want to turn on the computer? | *Niños, ¿quieren encender la computadora?* |
| Do you want to play on the computer? | *¿Quieren jugar en la computadora?* |
| What program do you want? | *¿Qué programa quieren?* |
| Can you see the screen? | *¿Pueden ver la pantalla?* |
| Olivia, take the mouse in your hand. | *Olivia, coge el ratón con tu mano.* |
| Put the CD in the computer. | *Pon el disco compacto[7] en la computadora.* |
| Where is the arrow? | *¿Dónde está la flecha?* |
| Move the curser over to the right. | *Mueve el cursor hacia la derecha.* |
| Click. | *Haz clic.* |

## IM-ing, chatting, and e-mailing

Although IM-ing and chat rooms certainly require some parental oversight, they can be excellent ways for your kids to communicate with Spanish-speaking kids all over the world.

| | |
|---|---|
| Jude, do you want to enter the chat room? | *Judas, ¿quieres entrar en la sala de charla?* |

---

7. Also *el CD* (with Spanish pronunciation, of course!)

| | |
|---|---|
| We have to enter your user name and password. | *Tenemos que poner tu nombre de usuario y tu contraseña.* |
| Let's see who's online. | *Vamos a ver quién está en línea.* |
| Oh, look, Patricia wants to chat with you! | *¡Ah, mira, Patricia quiere charlar contigo!* |
| Ask her where she's from and how old she is. | *Pregúntale de dónde es y cuántos años tiene.* |
| She's from Ecuador, great! Tell her what city you live in. | *Es de Ecuador, ¡qué bien! Dile en qué ciudad vives.* |
| Do you want to keep chatting or do you want to go off-line now? | *¿Quieres seguir charlando o quieres salir de línea ahora?* |
| Shall we write an e-mail to your friend Elena in Mexico? | *¿Le escribimos un correo electrónico a tu amiga Elena en México?* |
| Do you know her e-mail address? | *¿Sabes su dirección de correo electrónico?* |
| Open the e-mail program and click on "new message." | *Abre el programa de correo electrónico y haz clic en "mensaje nuevo."* |
| What a nice message! Now, click on "send." | *¡Qué mensaje más simpático! Ahora, haz clic en "enviar" ("mandar").* |
| Carlos wants to use the computer now. He wants to IM with Teresa. | *Carlos quiere usar la computadora ahora. Quiere hacer mensajería instantánea con Teresa.* |
| Carlos, is Teresa online right now? | *Carlos, ¿está Teresa en línea ahora?* |
| Great! Ask her if she wants to chat with you. | *¡Qué bien! Pregúntale si quiere charlar contigo.* |

# FAMILY EXCURSIONS

## GETTING OUT THE DOOR

aquarium, *el acuario*
beach, *la playa*
car race, *la carrera de autos*
countryside, *el campo*
dance performance, *el espectáculo
   de baile*
farm, *la granja, la finca*
game (sports), *el partido*
   baseball, *de béisbol*
   football, *de fútbol americano*
   soccer, *de fútbol*
ice show, *el espectáculo sobre hielo*
library, *la biblioteca*
mountains, *las montañas*

movies, *el cine*
museum, *el museo*
   children's, *de niños*
   fine arts, *de bellas artes*
   natural history, *de historia natural*
   science, *de ciencias*
park, *el parque*
playground, *el patio de recreo*
soccer practice, *la práctica de fútbol*
supermarket, *el supermercado*
swimming pool, *la piscina*
tennis match, *el partido de tenis*
theater, *el teatro*
zoo, *el zoológico*

### Let's go!

The following phrases are among the easiest to learn and the
most useful to know. "Let's go to . . ." is just "*Vamos a . . .*" Af-

ter that, it is just a matter of knowing where you are going: the playground, the library, the zoo, etc.

| Let's go. | *Vamos.* |
|---|---|
| Let's go to the zoo. | *Vamos al zoológico.* |

Note that *a el* gets contracted to *al*. Instead of *zoológico*, you can also say *zoo*. Just pronounce it as you would the English word *so*.

## Wanna go?

Perhaps you want to give your kid or kids some input into where you are going. If you are talking to one child, the construction is "*¿Quieres ir a . . .?*" If you are talking to two or more children, the question is "*¿Quieren ir a . . .?*"

| Saraí, do you want to go to the playground? | *Saraí, ¿quieres ir al patio de recreo?* |
|---|---|
| Kids, do you want to go to the zoo? | *Niños, ¿quieren ir al zoo?* |

You could also use the following:

| Olivia, would you like to go to the park? | *Olivia, ¿te gustaría ir al parque?* |
|---|---|
| Kids, would you like to go to the zoo? | *Niños, ¿les gustaría ir al zoo?* |

## Come along!

Oftentimes, you are going somewhere, say, to the supermarket, and you want to know if your child would like to come along. The easiest way to express this is to attach *conmigo* (with me), *con mami* (with mommy), *con papi* (with daddy), *con nosotros* (with us), or *con* anyone else to the above expressions.

| Olivia, do you want to go to the playground with me? | *Olivia, ¿quieres ir al patio de recreo conmigo?* |
|---|---|
| Bobby and Mary, do you want to go to the park with mommy? | *Bobby y María, ¿quieren ir al parque con mami?* |
| Kids, do you want to go to the zoo with us? | *Niños, ¿quieren ir al zoo con nosotros?* |

| | |
|---|---|
| Girls, do you want to go the zoo with your brother? | *Niñas, ¿quieren ir al zoo con su hermano?* |
| Marta, do you want to go to the library with your sister? | *Marta, ¿quieres ir a la biblioteca con tu hermana?* |
| Julian and David, do you want to go to the library with your uncles? | *Julián y David, ¿quieren ir a la biblioteca con sus tíos?* |

An alternative, and very common, way of saying the same thing is to use the verb *acompañar*, to accompany.

| | |
|---|---|
| Caroline, do want to accompany me? | *Carolina, ¿quieres acompañarme?* |
| Kids, I am going to the supermarket. Do you want to come along? | *Niños, voy al supermercado. ¿Quieren acompañarme?* |
| Girls, do you want to go to the playground with your aunt? | *Niñas, ¿quieren acompañar a su tía al patio de recreo?* |

## Getting ready to go

| | |
|---|---|
| We have to get ready to go now. | *Tenemos que prepararnos para irnos ahora.* |
| We have to leave in ten minutes. | *Tenemos que irnos en diez minutos.* |
| If we do not hurry we will be late. | *Si no nos apresuramos vamos a llegar tarde.* |
| If we are not ready soon we will miss the play. | *Si no estamos listos pronto, vamos a perder la obra.* |

## In the water

Most kids love water.

| | |
|---|---|
| Do you (all) want to go to the beach today? | *¿Quieres (quieren) ir a la playa hoy?* |
| Would you (all) like to go to the pool today? | *¿Te (Les) gustaría ir a la piscina hoy?* |
| Who wants to swim today? | *¿Quién quiere nadar[1] hoy?* |

---

1. You could say *bañarse* instead of *nadar*. *Bañarse* often refers to recreation in the water, while *nadar* refers to more serious swimming, such as lap swimming.

| | |
|---|---|
| We have to put on sunscreen. | *Tenemos que ponernos crema protectora.*[2] |
| Can you (all) put on your swimsuits, please? | *¿Puedes (Pueden) ponerte(se) el bañador,[3] por favor?* |
| Do you (all) have your beach toys? | *¿Tienes (Tienen) tus (sus) juguetes para la playa?* |
| Shall we take pails and shovels? | *¿Llevamos cubetas y palas?* |
| Let's take a beach umbrella and some beach chairs. | *Vamos a llevar una sombrilla y sillas para la playa.* |
| Don't forget your mask, fins, and snorkel. | *No olvides tu visor, tus aletas y tu snorkel.*[4] |

And, depending on the ages and swimming abilities of your kids:

| | |
|---|---|
| Don't (you all) go in the water without a big person. | *No entres (entren) en el agua sin una persona grande.* |

### Communing with nature

| | |
|---|---|
| Let's go for a walk in the countryside. | *Vamos de paseo al campo.* |
| Let's go see nature. | *Vamos a ver la naturaleza.* |
| Ellen, look at the trees. | *Elena, mira los árboles.* |
| Boys, look at the mountains in the distance. | *Niños, miren las montañas a lo lejos.* |
| Look, everyone, there is a squirrel. | *Miren, hay una ardilla.* |
| The leaves are changing color. | *Las hojas están cambiando de color.* |
| The sun is setting. | *El sol se está poniendo.* |
| Kids, look at the sunset. | *Niños, miren la puesta del sol.* |
| Robert, look at the sunrise. | *Roberto, mira la salida del sol.* |
| The moon is rising. | *La luna está saliendo.* |
| The stars are shining. | *Brillan las estrellas.* |
| Can you all see the bats? | *¿Pueden ver los murciélagos?* |
| Let's follow this path. | *Vamos a seguir este camino.* |
| Let's climb the hill. | *Vamos a subir la colina.* |
| Let's go into the woods. | *Vamos a entrar en el bosque.* |

---

2. Suntan lotion would be *el bronceador.*
3. Also, *el traje de baño.*
4. *Snorkel* is most often pronounced as if spelled *esnorkel.*

| | |
|---|---|
| There are no bears in these woods. | *No hay osos aquí en el bosque.* |
| There are deer around here. | *Hay ciervos⁵ por aquí.* |

(See the "Our Animal Friends" chapter, or look up specific animals in the glossary.)

| | |
|---|---|
| Edward, are you tired? | *Eduardo, ¿estás cansado?* |
| Do you want me to carry you? | *¿Quieres que te lleve?* |
| Do you want to sit on my shoulders? | *¿Te llevo en hombros?* |
| Who wants to go camping this weekend? | *¿Quién quiere acampar este fin de semana?* |
| Let's look for the tent. | *Vamos a buscar la tienda de campaña.* |

---

5. Also, *venados*.

# CAR, BUS, TRAIN, PLANE

**KEY VOCABULARY:**

car seat (for kids), *el asiento de niño*
horn, *la bocina*
seat belt, *el cinturón de seguridad*
seat (car), *el asiento de carro*
    backseat, *el asiento de atrás*
    driver's seat, *el asiento del*
      *conductor*
    front seat, *el asiento delantero*
    passenger seat, *el asiento del*
      *pasajero*

steering wheel, *el volante*
window (car), *la ventana,*
    *la ventanilla*
windshield, *el parabrisas*
windshield wiper, *el limpiaparabrisas*

to brake, *frenar*
to drive, *manejar*
to stop, *parar*
to turn, *dar la vuelta*

## Traveling by car

Marcela, get in your car seat, please. | *Marcela, métete en tu asiento de carro, por favor.*

Girls, get in the car, please. | *Niñas, métanse en el carro, por favor.*
Adam, fasten your seat belt, please. | *Adán, ponte el cinturón de seguridad, por favor.*

Fasten your seat belts, everybody. | *Todos, pónganse el cinturón.*
Anthony, can you put up your window? | *Antonio, ¿puedes subir la ventana?*

Is there too much wind back there? | *¿Hay demasiado aire allí atrás?*
We are going to stop soon to eat. | *Vamos a parar pronto para comer.*
We are going to be there in one hour. | *Vamos a llegar en una hora.*
We are almost there. | *Ya casi llegamos.*

## Planes and boats and trains

Of course, there are many other ways to travel: *en tren* (by train), *en barco* (by boat), *en autobús* (by bus), *en avión* (by plane), and even *caminando* (walking).

Are we going by bus or by train? | *¿Vamos en autobús o en tren?*
We need to purchase tickets. | *Tenemos que comprar boletos.*

| | |
|---|---|
| Did you (all) pack your suitcases? | *¿Hiciste (Hicieron) las maletas?* |
| The train is moving! | *¡El tren se está moviendo!* |
| The bus is stopping! | *¡El autobús está parando!* |
| The plane is taking off! | *¡El avión está despegando!* |
| The plane is landing! | *¡El avión está aterrizando!* |

## HOLIDAYS

**KEY VOCABULARY:**

bat, *el murciélago*
dragon, *el dragón*
fairy, *el hada*
ghost, *el fantasma*
Halloween costumes, *los disfraces de la Noche de Brujas*
king, *el rey*
monster, *el monstruo*
mummy, *la momia*

prince, *el príncipe*
princess, *la princesa*
queen, *la reina*
robot, *el robot*
skeleton, *el esqueleto*
vampire, *el vampiro*
warlock, *el brujo*
werewolf, *el hombre lobo*
witch, *la bruja*

### Birthdays

| | |
|---|---|
| Charles, when is your birthday? | *Carlos, ¿cuándo es tu cumpleaños?* |
| How old are you going to be? | *¿Cuántos años vas a cumplir?* |
| Are you going to have a birthday party? | *¿Vas a tener una fiesta de cumpleaños?* |
| Do you want to have a birthday party? | *¿Quieres tener una fiesta de cumpleaños?* |
| Do you want to invite a few friends? | *¿Quieres invitar a unos cuantos amiguitos?* |
| Whom do you want to invite? | *¿A quién quieres invitar?* |
| We should invite Paul and Martha. | *Deberíamos invitar a Pablo y Marta.* |
| Do you want a birthday cake with candles? | *¿Quieres un pastel de cumpleaños con velas?* |
| Make a wish and blow out the candles. | *Pide un deseo y apaga las velas.* |
| Blow! | *¡Sóplale!* |
| Happy birthday! | *¡Feliz cumpleaños!* |
| Do you want party hats? | *¿Quieres gorritos de fiesta?* |
| Who wants cake? | *¿Quién quiere pastel?* |
| Who wants ice cream with their cake? | *¿Quién quiere helado con su pastel?* |
| It's time to open presents. | *Es hora de abrir los regalos.* |
| Can your little sister help you open the presents? | *¿Puede tu hermanita ayudarte a abrir los regalos?* |

| | |
|---|---|
| Guess what it is. | *Adivina qué es.* |
| What a beautiful present! | *¡Qué regalo más hermoso!* |
| Who is that from? | *¿Quién te lo dio?* |
| Don't forget to say thank you. | *No se te olvide dar las gracias.* |
| Don't forget to thank your uncle for the present. | *No se te olvide darle las gracias a tu tío por el regalo.* |
| Can you put the paper in the trash (recycling)? | *¿Puedes meter el papel en la basura (el reciclaje)?* |
| Say goodbye to your friends. | *Despídete de tus amigos.* |

You can sing "Happy Birthday to You" (to the same tune) as follows:[6]

| | |
|---|---|
| Happy Birthday to you | *Feliz cumpleaños a ti* |
| Happy Birthday to you | *Feliz cumpleaños a ti* |
| Happy Birthday dear Olivia | *Feliz cumpleaños, querida Olivia* |
| Happy Birthday to you | *Feliz cumpleaños a ti* |

## Christmas, Hanukkah, and the New Year

| | |
|---|---|
| Merry Christmas! | *¡Feliz Navidad!* |
| Happy Hanukkah! | *¡Feliz Hanukkah!* |
| Christmas is a Christian holiday. | *La Navidad es un día festivo cristiano.* |
| Christmas is the birthday of Jesus. | *La Navidad es el cumpleaños de Jesús.* |
| Hanukkah is a Jewish holiday. | *Hanukkah es una fiesta judía.* |
| Hanukkah is the holiday of the lights. | *Hanukkah es la fiesta de las luces.* |
| Each day of Hanukkah another candle is lit. | *Cada día de Hanukkah se enciende otra vela.* |
| I love Christmastime. | *Me encanta las Navidades.* |
| It's Christmas eve. | *Es Nochebuena.* |
| We are going to midnight mass. | *Vamos a la misa de gallo.* |
| Tomorrow is Christmas day. | *Mañana es el día de Navidad.* |
| Let's go find a Christmas tree. | *Vamos a buscar un árbol de Navidad.* |
| George, you can help pick the tree. | *Jorge, puedes ayudar a escoger el árbol.* |
| Kids, you can help decorate the tree. | *Niños, pueden ayudar a decorar el árbol.* |

---

6. In Mexico and some other areas of Latin America, the traditional birthday song is *Las mañanitas.*

| | |
|---|---|
| Angela, can you put this ornament on the tree? | *Ángela, ¿puedes poner este ornamento[7] en el árbol?* |
| Mary, can you help me put the lights on the tree? | *María, ¿puedes ayudarme a poner las luces en el árbol?* |
| Let's go see Santa Claus. | *Vamos a ver a Santa Claus.[8]* |
| Let's send Christmas cards. | *Vamos a enviar las tarjetas de Navidad.* |
| Claire, do you want to leave some cookies for Santa? | *Clarita, ¿quieres dejar algunas galletas para Santa Claus?* |
| Kids, do you want to leave some carrots for Santa's reindeer? | *Niños, ¿quieren dejar zanahorias para los renos de Santa Claus?* |
| I want to see Rudolph the Red-Nosed Reindeer. | *Quiero ver a Rodolfo el Reno de la Nariz Roja.* |
| Where does Santa live? | *¿Dónde vive Santa Claus?* |
| Santa's workshop is at the North Pole. | *El taller de Santa Claus está en el polo norte.* |
| He has many elves to help him make toys. | *Tiene muchos elfos para ayudarlo a hacer juguetes.* |
| He flies through the air with his sled and his reindeer. | *Vuela por el aire con su trineo y renos.* |
| He comes down the chimney with his bag of toys. | *Baja por la chimenea con su saco de juguetes.* |
| We are going Christmas caroling. | *Vamos a cantar villancicos de casa en casa.[9]* |

## Easter

| | |
|---|---|
| When is Easter? | *¿Cuando es el Día de Pascua?* |
| When is Holy Week? | *¿Cuando es la Semana Santa?* |
| Easter is in three weeks, more or less. | *La Pascua es en tres semanas, más o menos.* |
| Who wants to color eggs? | *¿Quién quiere colorear huevos?* |

---

7. Also, *la decoración.*

8. "Claus" is pronounced "close" (as in "close to home"). "Santa Claus" is more common in some countries, such as Mexico (primarily because of U.S. influence), but "Papá Noel" is more common in many others.

9. *Los villancicos* are Christmas carols. *Las canciones navideñas* are Christmas songs in general.

| | |
|---|---|
| Tonight the Easter bunny will come and hide the eggs, and tomorrow we will look for them. | *Esta noche el conejo de Pascua vendrá a esconder los huevos y mañana los buscaremos.* |
| Let's look for the Easter eggs. | *Vamos a buscar los huevos de Pascua.* |
| Julie, do you have a chocolate bunny? | *Julia, ¿tienes un conejito de chocolate?* |
| Girls, do you have your Easter baskets? | *Niñas, ¿tienen sus canastas de Pascua?* |

## Thanksgiving

Thanksgiving is our favorite holiday of the year. Winter is approaching. The leaves are almost off the trees. There is a chill in the air. The fire is burning in the woodstove. Family and friends stop by. And then there is the food.

| | |
|---|---|
| It's Thanksgiving today! | *¡Hoy es el Día de Acción de Gracias!* |
| We are making turkey with stuffing. | *Estamos preparando pavo relleno.* |
| We are also going to eat cranberry sauce and sweet potatoes. | *También vamos a comer salsa de arándano y camotes.* |
| Anyone want more mashed potatoes with gravy? | *¿Alguien quiere más puré de papas con salsa?* |
| Ernest, would you like mince pie or pumpkin pie? | *Ernesto, ¿te gustaría pastel de frutas picadas o de calabaza?* |
| Children, which pie do you want? | *Niños, ¿qué pastel quieren?* |
| Sabrina, which do you want? | *Sabrina, ¿cuál quieres?* |

(See the glossary for more food words.)

## Halloween

> **CULTURAL NOTE**
> In the United States, we celebrate Halloween on the evening of October 31. In Latin America, there are a number of different traditions that celebrate the dead, including *Noche Santificada*, *El Día de Todos los Santos*, and *el Día de los Difuntos* or *El Día de los Muertos*. The dates may or may not correspond to Halloween. (In many places, *el Día de los Muertos* is on November 2. Spanish speakers familiar with the U.S. holiday typically refer to it as *Halloween* or *la Noche de Brujas* (night of witches). The custom of trick-or-treating is also practiced in some Latin American countries.

| | |
|---|---|
| Halloween is coming. | *Halloween viene.* |
| Anne, are you going to dress up? | *Ana, ¿vas a disfrazarte?* |
| Claudia and Daniel, are you going to dress up? | *Claudia y Daniel, ¿van a disfrazarse?* |
| Anne, what are you going to dress up as? | *Ana, ¿de qué te vas a disfrazar?* |
| Daniel, do you want me to make you a costume? | *Daniel, ¿quieres que te haga un disfraz?* |
| Claudia and Daniel, do you want me to make you costumes? | *Claudia y Daniel, ¿quieren que les haga un disfraz?* |
| Ellen, are you going to dress up as a witch? | *Ellen, ¿vas a disfrazarte de bruja?* |

(See the glossary for Halloween costumes.)

| | |
|---|---|
| Are you all going trick-or-treating? | *¿Van a ir a pedir caramelos?* |
| Eve, do you have a bag to collect candy? | *Eva, ¿tienes una bolsa para recoger caramelos?* |
| Daniel, take your little sister with you. | *Daniel, lleva a tu hermanita contigo.* |
| Watch out for cars! | *¡Cuidado con los carros!* |
| Hold hands when crossing the street. | *Agárrense de la mano para cruzar la calle.* |
| Claudia, don't go in any houses. | *Claudia, no entres en ninguna casa.* |

| | |
|---|---|
| Claudia y Daniel, don't go in any houses. | *Claudia y Daniel, no entren en ninguna casa.* |
| You must come back at eight. | *Hay que regresar a las ocho.* |

## Other holidays

| | |
|---|---|
| Independence Day | *El Día de la Independencia* |
| Labor Day | *El Día del Trabajo* |
| Three Kings Day | *El Día de los Reyes Magos* |
| Valentine's Day | *El Día de San Valentín*[10] |

10. Also *el Día del Amor y la Amistad* or *el Día de los Enamorados.*

# IN THE KITCHEN

## COOKING

**KEY VOCABULARY:**

bowl, *el tazón*
cut, *una cortada*
oven, *el horno*
pan, *el sartén*

refrigerator, *el refrigerador*
scrape, *una raspada*
stove, *la estufa*

Some kids love to cook. With their help it may only take you twice as long to prepare the food.

| | |
|---|---|
| Noah, do want to help me? | *Noé, ¿quieres ayudarme?* |
| Noah, put on the apron. | *Noé, ponte el delantal.* |
| Caroline and Saraí, do you want to help me prepare supper? | *Carolina y Saraí, ¿quieren ayudarme a preparar la cena?* |
| Girls, wash your hands, please. | *Niñas, lávense las manos, por favor.* |
| Let's make cookies. | *Vamos a hacer galletas.* |
| Noah, can you put the flour in the bowl, please? | *Noé, ¿puedes poner la harina en el tazón,[1] por favor?* |
| Saraí, can you put the milk in? | *Saraí, ¿puedes meter la leche?* |
| Caroline, can you crack the eggs and put them in? | *Carolina, ¿puedes romper los huevos y meterlos?* |

---

1. You can also use *bol* or *plato hondo*.

| | |
|---|---|
| Can you mix the milk, eggs, and flour? | *¿Puedes mezclar la leche, los huevos y la harina?* |
| Careful with the milk! | *¡Cuidado con la leche!*[2] |
| The milk spilled. | *La leche se derramó.* |
| Let's clean up the milk. | *Vamos a recoger la leche.* |
| Carolina, can you stir the batter, please? | *Carolina, ¿puedes remover la pasta, por favor?* |
| Jude, can you get me a small pan? | *Judas, ¿puedes buscarme un sartén pequeño?* |
| Let's beat the batter. | *Vamos a batir la pasta.* |
| Let's put the dough in the pan. | *Vamos a meter la masa en el molde.* |
| Let's put the bread in the oven. | *Vamos a meter el pan al horno.* |
| Let's bake the bread. | *Vamos a hornear el pan.* |

## It's hot!

| | |
|---|---|
| I'm going to turn the oven on. | *Voy a encender el horno.* |
| The stove is on. | *La estufa*[3] *está encendida.* |
| Careful, the pan is hot. | *Cuidado, el sartén está caliente.* |
| Sarah, don't go near the stove. | *Sara, no te acerques a la estufa.* |
| Kids, don't go near the oven. | *Niños, no se acerquen al horno.* |
| Noah, don't touch the pan. | *Noé, no toques el sartén.* |
| Kids, don't touch the oven. | *Niños, no toquen el horno.* |
| Don't burn yourself. | *No te quemes.* |
| Don't burn yourselves. | *No se quemen.* |
| It's OK. The pan is cool now. | *Está bien. El sartén ya está frío.* |
| It's OK to touch it now. | *Se puede tocar ahora.* |

---

2. As in English, this is simply a common abbreviated way to say "be careful," or, literally, "have care" (*ten cuidado*).

3. In Spain, this would be *la candela*.

## MEALTIME

Mealtime has lots of vocabulary, and terms can vary quite a bit from region to region. This should give you a good start, though. See the glossary as well.

### Breakfast

bread, *el pan*
butter, *la mantequilla*
cream, *la crema*
cereal, *el cereal*
    bowl of cereal, *el tazón de cereal*
    cream of wheat, *cereal de crema de trigo*
    oatmeal, *la avena*
egg, *el huevo*
    fried egg, *huevo frito*
    scrambled egg, *huevo revuelto*
french toast, *el pan francés*
jelly, *la mermelada*

juice, *el jugo*[4]
    orange juice, *jugo de naranja*
margarine, *la margarina*
milk, *la leche*
muffin, *el panecillo*
oil, *el aceite*
pancake, *el panqueque*
peanut butter, *crema de cacahuate*
sausage, *la salchicha*
syrup, *el jarabe*
toast, *la tostada*
water, *el agua*
wiener, *la salchicha*

### Fruits and vegetables

apple, *la manzana*
    apple peel, *la cáscara de manzana*
    applesauce, *el puré de manzana*
banana, *el plátano*
    banana peel, *la cáscara de plátano*
beans (green), *los ejotes*
beans (kidney, etc.), *los frijoles*
berry, *la mora*
corn, *el maíz*
    corn on the cob, *el maíz en la mazorca*

cranberry, *el arándano*
grape, *la uva*
lemon, *el limón*
lime, *la lima*
mango, *el mango*
melon, *el melón*
nut, *la nuez*
orange, *la naranja*
peach, *el durazno*
pear, *la pera*
peas, *los guisantes*

---

4. In Spain you would say *zumo* instead of *jugo*.

plum, *la ciruela*
prune (dried), *la ciruela pasa*
raisin, *la pasa*
raspberry, *la frambuesa*

rice, *el arroz*
strawberry, *la fresa*
watermelon, *la sandía*

## Lunch and dinner

beef, *la carne de res*
cake, *el pastel*
chicken, *el pollo*
corn chip, *el totopo*
cracker, *la galleta salada*
fish, *el pescado*
ham, *el jamón*
hamburger, *la hamburguesa*
hot dog, *un hot dog*
macaroni and cheese, *macarrones
   con queso*
meat, *la carne*
pasta, *la pasta*
pie, *el pastel*[5]
pork, *el puerco*
   pork chops, *las chuletas de puerco*

ribs, *las costillas*
sandwich, *el sandwich, el bocadillo*
   cheese sandwich, *el sandwich
     de queso*
   grilled cheese sandwich, *el sandwich
     de queso fundido*
snack, *la merienda*
soup, *la sopa*
   chicken noodle soup, *la sopa de
     fideo con pollo*
   chicken soup, *la sopa de pollo*
   mushroom soup, *la sopa de
     champiñones*
   tomato soup, *la sopa de tomate*

## Dessert

cookie, *la galleta*
ice cream, *el helado*
   chocolate, *chocolate*
   in a cone, *en un barquillo*
   strawberry, *fresa*
   vanilla, *vainilla*
   with chocolate syrup, *con salsa de chocolate*

---

5. Also, *el pay*, pronounced as in the English, *pie*.

## Meals of the day

Though it varies with country and region, the usual meals of the day are *desayuno* (breakfast), *comida* (the large midday meal), and *cena* (supper). *Almuerzo* is a light midday meal (lunch) that we *norteamericanos* tend to eat.

| | |
|---|---|
| breakfast | *el desayuno* |
| lunch | *el almuerzo* |
| midday meal | *la comida* |
| dinner | *la cena* |

With kids, there are snacks.

| | |
|---|---|
| snack | *la merienda* |

*Comida* is also the generic word for food. *Comer* is to eat, in general, and it is also the verb you would use to refer to eating the *comida*, the large midday meal. *Almorzar* is to have lunch. *Desayunar* is to eat breakfast, and *cenar* is to eat dinner.

| | |
|---|---|
| Let's eat. | *Vamos a comer.* |
| What do you (all) want to have for breakfast? | *¿Qué quieres (quieren) desayunar?* |
| We already had lunch. | *Ya almorzamos.* |
| We're going to have chicken for dinner. | *Vamos a cenar pollo.* |

## Ready to eat?

| | |
|---|---|
| Louis, are you hungry? | *Luis, ¿tienes hambre?* |
| Louis y Claudia, are you thirsty? | *Luis y Claudia, ¿tienen sed?* |
| Louis, are you ready to eat? | *Luis, ¿estás listo para comer?* |
| Girls, are you ready to eat? | *Niñas, ¿están listas para comer?* |
| Who wants to eat? | *¿Quién quiere comer?* |

## The menu

Mary sometimes tells the kids that this is not a restaurant, that what is for dinner is what she is cooking. The truth is that she often solicits suggestions. And sometimes it *is* a restaurant.

|  |  |
|---|---|
| Cecilia, what do you want to eat? | *Cecilia, ¿qué quieres comer?* |
| Kids, what do you want to eat? | *Niños, ¿qué quieren comer?* |
| There is macaroni and cheese or rice and chicken. | *Hay macarrones con queso o arroz con pollo.* |
| Cecilia, what do you want to drink: milk, juice, or water? | *Cecilia, ¿qué quieres tomar: leche, jugo o agua?* |
| There is orange juice and tomato juice. | *Hay jugo de naranja y jugo de tomate.* |

## Setting the table, etc.

|  |  |
|---|---|
| Who wants to set the table? | *¿Quién quiere poner la mesa?* |
| Daniela, can you put plates on the table? | *Daniela, ¿puedes poner platos en la mesa?* |
| Girls, can you put utensils (silverware) on the table? | *Niñas, ¿pueden poner los cubiertos en la mesa?* |
| Homer, do you want to serve the food? | *Homero, ¿quieres servir la comida?* |

## Mealtime manners

|  |  |
|---|---|
| Can you pass me the salt, please? | *Puedes pasarme la sal, por favor?* |
| Monica, do you like the chicken? | *Mónica, ¿te gusta el pollo?* |
| Girls, do you like the rice? | *Niñas, ¿les gusta el arroz?* |
| Who wants more pasta? | *¿Quién quiere más pasta?* |

## Dessert!

|  |  |
|---|---|
| Who wants dessert? | *¿Quién quiere postre?* |
| Who is ready for dessert? | *¿Quién está listo para el postre?* |
| George, do you want some ice cream? | *Jorge, ¿quieres un poco de helado?* |
| What flavor do you want: chocolate, vanilla, or strawberry? | *¿De qué sabor lo quieres: chocolate, vainilla o fresa?* |
| Do you want some chocolate syrup on your ice cream? | *¿Quieres salsa de chocolate en tu helado?* |
| Kids, do you want some cake? | *Niños, ¿quieren pastel?* |
| We have cookies or fruit pie. | *Tenemos galletas o pastel de fruta.* |

## Kitchen cleanup

Who wants to clear the table?

James, do you want to help me to wash the dishes?

¿Quién quiere recoger la mesa?

Jaime, ¿quieres ayudarme a lavar los platos?

# BEDTIME

## GOODNIGHT!

The verb for going to bed is *acostarse*, which also means *to lie down*.

| | |
|---|---|
| Kids, it's time to go to bed. | *Niños, es hora de acostarse.* |
| Jorge, it is time for you to go to bed. | *Jorge, es hora de acostarte.* |

You can also express it just as in English:

| | |
|---|---|
| It is time to go to bed. | *Es hora de ir a la cama.* |
| It is time to sleep. | *Es hora de dormir.* |

A nap, of course, is *una siesta*.

| | |
|---|---|
| It is time to nap. | *Es hora de dormir la siesta.* |
| If you can't sleep, son, just try to rest. | *Si no puedes dormir, hijo, trata de descansar.* |

## Why do I have to go to bed?

The reasons for going to bed are various.

| | |
|---|---|
| Because it is time. | *Porque ya es hora.* |
| Look at the clock. | *Mira el reloj.* |

| | |
|---|---|
| It is already nine o'clock. | *Ya son las nueve.* |
| Because it is very late. | *Porque es muy tarde.* |
| Because you are tired. | *Porque estás cansado.* |
| Because you are sleepy. | *Porque tienes sueño.* |
| We let you stay up very late tonight already. | *Ya te dejamos estar despierto hasta muy tarde esta noche.* |
| If you want to stay up late in the future you have to go to bed when it is time. | *Si quieres estar despierto hasta tarde en el futuro, tienes que ir a la cama cuando es hora.* |

## Getting ready for bed

See the "In the Bathroom" section for brushing teeth, etc.

| | |
|---|---|
| Marcela, will you put on your pajamas, please?. | *Marcela, ¿quieres ponerte el pijama,[1] por favor?* |
| Boys, can you put on your pajamas? | *Niños, ¿pueden ponerse el pijama?* |
| It is going to be cold tonight. | *Va a hacer frío esta noche.* |
| Will you (all) put on something warm? | *¿Quieres (quieren) ponerte (ponerse) algo calentito?* |
| Marcela, please give your uncle a kiss and tell him goodnight. | *Marcela, dale un beso a tu tío y dile buenas noches, por favor.* |
| Do you (all) want to read a story before bed? | *¿Quieres (quieren) leer un cuento antes de ir a la cama?* |
| If you (all) get ready for bed really fast, we will have time for a story. | *Si puedes (pueden) prepararte (prepararse) para la cama muy rápido, tendremos tiempo para leer un cuento.* |

## Getting into bed

| | |
|---|---|
| Fred, get into bed. | *Federico, métete en la cama.* |
| Girls, get under the sheets. | *Niñas, métanse debajo de las sábanas.* |
| Fred, lie down, please. | *Federico, acuéstate, por favor.* |
| Cover yourself with the blanket. | *Tápate con la manta.* |
| Here's your pillow. | *Aquí está tu almohada.* |

---

1. In some countries, people say *la piyama*.

| | |
|---|---|
| Turn off the light, please. | *Apaga la luz, por favor.* |
| I am going to turn off the light. | *Voy a apagar la luz.* |
| Roger, go to sleep. | *Rogelio, duérmete.* |

---

### CULTURAL NOTE

Here is a little lullaby poem. (It sort of rhymes in Spanish.)

| | |
|---|---|
| Go to sleep, my child | *Duérmete, mi hijo (hija)* |
| Go to sleep, my sunshine | *Duérmete, mi sol* |
| Go to sleep, little piece | *Duérmete, pedacito* |
| Of my heart. | *De mi corazón* |

---

## Last-minute concerns

| | |
|---|---|
| Do you (all) want the night-light? | *¿Quieres (Quieren) la lamparita?* |
| Do you (all) want some water for your night table? | *¿Quieres (Quieren) un poco de agua para tu (su) mesita?* |
| Do you (all) want me to leave the door open a little bit? | *¿Quieres (quieren) que deje la puerta un poco abierta?* |
| Do you (all) want some music? | *¿Quieres (quieren) un poco de música?* |
| Do you want me to snuggle with you a little? | *¿Quieres que me acurruque contigo un poco?* |
| Do you want me to rub your back for a few minutes? | *¿Quieres que te frote la espalda unos cuantos minutos?* |
| Do you want me to tell you (all) a short story? | *¿Quieres(Quieren) que te (les) cuente un cuentito?* |
| Girls, you can talk for ten minutes. | *Niñas, pueden hablar por diez minutos.* |

---

## Saying goodnight

| | |
|---|---|
| Goodnight. | *Buenas noches.* |
| Sweet dreams (you all). | *Que sueñes (sueñen) con los angelitos.* (Literally, "May you dream with the little angels.") |
| Until tomorrow. | *Hasta mañana.* |
| Give me a kiss, please. | *Dame un beso, por favor.* |
| Give me a hug. | *Dame un abrazo.* |

| | |
|---|---|
| I will be just downstairs. | *Voy a estar justo abajo.* |
| Dad and I will be in our bedroom. | *Papi y yo vamos a estar en nuestro dormitorio.* |
| I love you (all). | *Te (Los, Las) quiero.* |

## Dreams (and nightmares)

To dream is *soñar*. A dream is *un sueño*, and a nightmare is *una pesadilla*. To dream about someone or something is *soñar con*.

| | |
|---|---|
| Are you dreaming? | *¿Estás soñando?* |
| What were you dreaming about? | *¿Con qué estabas soñando?* |
| Were you dreaming about your school? | *¿Estabas soñando con tu escuela?* |
| Tell me about your dream. | *Cuéntame tu sueño.* |
| Did you have a nightmare? | *¿Tuviste una pesadilla?* |
| I will stay with you for a little while. | *Me quedo contigo un ratito.* |

## STORY TIME

Story time can be anytime. Reading presents great opportunities for conversation with kids. However, there are far more stories than the kinds that you get from books. Kids love made-up stories and love to make up stories. Particularly at bedtime, when the lights went out, our kids would ask for a *"cuento sin libro."* (Of course, they were stalling, but why not take  advantage of it?) At some point, kids want stories about you, about when you were small, or about their relatives or even about themselves when they were small. And then there are stories about the future—the near future as in what we are going to do tomorrow or when we go on vacation, and the more distant future, as in what it will be like when they grow up. All of these stories are wonderful opportunities for conversation with your kids. Like most conversations, interactive storytelling is often a matter of asking the right questions.

### Read me a story

There are many opportunities for reading. The key is to make reading a two-way experience. As you read, ask a lot of questions. This aids both comprehension and expression.

| | |
|---|---|
| Alice, do you want me to read you a story? | *Alicia, ¿Quieres que te lea un cuento?* |
| Girls, do you want me to read you a book? | *Niñas, ¿quieren que les lea un libro?* |
| What book do you (all) want? | *¿Qué libro quieres (quieren)?* |
| Claire, go and get a book. | *Clara, ve a buscar un libro.* |
| Boys, go and get a book. | *Niños, vayan a buscar un libro.* |
| Boys, each one of you can choose a book. | *Niños, cada uno puede escoger un libro.* |
| Girls, each one of you can choose a story. | *Niñas, cada una puede escoger un cuento.* |
| Where are we going to read? | *¿Dónde vamos a leer?* |
| You can sit on my lap. | *Puedes sentarte en mi regazo.* |
| You can sit on this side and you on the other side. | *Tú puedes sentarte en este lado y tú en el otro lado.* |

| | |
|---|---|
| You can sit on the right and you on the left. | *Tú puedes sentarte a la derecha y tú a la izquierda.* |
| Who wants to turn the page? | *¿Quién quiere cambiar la página?*[2] |
| Robert, are you ready to begin? | *Roberto, ¿estás listo para empezar?* |
| Girls, are you ready for the next chapter? | *Niñas, ¿están listas para el próximo capítulo?* |

## What's happening?

Asking questions as you proceed through a story is a good way to stimulate conversation. One way to do this is to take a line from the story and ask why.

From story: *Pablo saltó del puente.* (Paul jumped from the bridge.)
Question: *¿Por qué saltó Pablo del puente?* (Why did Paul jump from the bridge?)
From story: *Paula empezó a llorar.* (Paula began to cry.)
Question: *¿Por qué empezó a llorar?* (Why did she begin to cry?)

In this spirit, there are lots of questions one can ask about the story.

| | |
|---|---|
| What is happening in this picture? | *¿Qué está pasando en este dibujo?* |
| What do you (all) think is going to happen now? | *¿Qué crees (creen) que va a pasar ahora?* |
| Who is this person? | *¿Quién es esta persona?* |
| What is she going to do? | *¿Qué va a hacer?* |
| Why did he do that? | *¿Por qué hizo eso?* |
| Why is she dressed like that? | *¿Por qué está vestida así?* |
| Why are they running? | *¿Por qué están corriendo?* |
| What colors are there on this page? | *¿Qué colores hay en esta página?* |
| What do you (all) see in this picture? | *¿Qué ves (ven) en este dibujo?* |
| Is she happy? | *¿Está contenta?* |

---

2. Also, *darle la vuelta a la página* or, in some places, *pasar la página.*

# ESPECIALLY FOR BABY

Baby has her own set of vocabulary and expressions. Naturally, since baby talk is such an intimate and familiar form of conversation, there are many, many regional variations. Here are the most common words and expressions. (See also the glossary under "Baby.")

## Diaper duty

| | |
|---|---|
| Do you have a wet diaper? | *¿Tienes un pañal mojado?* |
| Do you have a dirty diaper? | *¿Tienes un pañal sucio?* |
| Let me see. | *Déjame ver.* |
| Let me check your diaper. | *Déjame ver tu pañal.* |
| Ah, it's wet. | *Ay, está mojado.* |
| It's OK. | *Está bien.* |
| I am going to change your diaper. | *Voy a cambiarte el pañal.* |
| I am going to put on a clean diaper. | *Voy a ponerte un pañal limpio.* |
| I am going to put on a dry diaper. | *Voy a ponerte un pañal seco.* |
| Would you like a little cream? | *¿Te gustaría un poco de crema?* |
| Do you want some powder? | *¿Quieres un poco de talco?* |
| I am going to powder your bottom. | *Voy a ponerte talco en la colita.*[1] |

---

1. Also, *las pompas* or *las pompitas*.

## Feeding time

| | |
|---|---|
| Are you hungry? | *¿Tienes hambre?* |
| Are you thirsty? | *¿Tienes sed?* |
| Do you want to drink something? | *¿Quieres tomar algo?* |
| Do you want your bottle? | *¿Quieres tu biberón?* |
| Do you want milk? | *¿Quieres leche?* |
| Do you want water? | *¿Quieres agua?* |
| Do you want to eat? | *¿Quieres comer?* |
| I have to put on your bib. | *Tengo que ponerte el babero.* |
| Open your mouth, please. | *Abre la boca, por favor.* |
| Ummmm, how good. | *Umm, que rico.* |
| Do you want more? | *¿Quieres más?* |
| Don't throw your plate. | *No tires el plato.* |
| Don't throw your food. | *No tires la comida.* |
| Here is your spoon. | *Aquí tienes tu cuchara.* |
| You have food all over your face. | *Tienes comida por toda la cara.*[2] |
| There is food everywhere. | *Hay comida en todas partes.* |
| Are you having fun? | *¿Te estás divirtiendo?* |
| Very good. You ate a lot. | *Muy bien. Comiste mucho.* |

## Going for a walk

| | |
|---|---|
| Do you want to go for a walk? | *¿Quieres ir de paseo?* |
| I am going to put you in your carriage (stroller). | *Voy a meterte en tu cochecito.* |
| Let me get you out of your carriage. | *Déjame sacarte de tu cochecito.* |

## Baby clothes

For the most part, baby clothes have the same names as kid clothes. There are, however, a couple of exceptions.

| | |
|---|---|
| I am going to put you in your snowsuit. | *Voy a ponerte el traje para la nieve.* |

---

2. You could also say to a baby with food smeared all over his or her face, *Éstas todo batido (Éstas toda batida).*

And then there is the ubiquitous one-piece (or "onesie"), that undershirt sort of thing that snaps in the crotch.

| | |
|---|---|
| Oh, you need another one-piece. | *Ah, necesitas otra camiseta.* |

## When baby fusses

| | |
|---|---|
| Daughter, don't cry. | *Hija, no llores.* |
| Do you want your pacifier? | *¿Quieres tu chupón?* |
| Do you want me to hold you? | *¿Quieres que te coja en brazos?* |
| Do you want me to rock you? | *¿Quieres que te meza?* |
| I'm going to rock you a little. | *Voy a mecerte un poco.* |
| Do you want me to sing you a song? | *¿Quieres que te cante una canción?* |
| Do you want a toy? | *¿Quieres un juguete?* |
| Do you want your rattle? | *¿Quieres tu sonajero?* |

## Moving about

| | |
|---|---|
| Are you going to crawl? | *¿Vas a gatear?* |
| Are you going to roll over? | *¿Vas a darte la vuelta?* |
| Are you going to try to stand? | *¿Vas a tratar de pararte?* |
| Walk to daddy. | *Camina hacia papi.* |

## Beddie-bye

| | |
|---|---|
| Are you sleepy? | *¿Tienes sueño?* |
| Do you want to sleep? | *¿Quieres dormir?* |
| Go to sleep. | *Duérmete.* |
| I am going to put you in your crib. | *Voy a meterte en tu cuna.* |

# A QUICK COURSE IN
# SPANISH PRONUNCIATION

Knowing the rudiments of pronunciation is important for both reading to your child and for speech. Of course, it is not important that you speak accent-free Spanish. Your child will have other sources of fluent Spanish around, such as television, music, books on tape, or child care. Your child will quickly figure out whose accent to emulate and even come to correct you on occasion. In the meantime, your speech is providing vocabulary and basic grammatical structures. This is true even if your pronunciation is not perfect and even if your grammar experiences occasional lapses. Most importantly, you are providing inspiration.

The great thing about Spanish is that its pronunciation is very straightforward. With few exceptions, English contains all of the sounds that exist in Spanish, or close approximations of them. In addition, Spanish spelling is both regular and phonetic. Spanish dictionaries do not have pronunciation guides because the pronunciation is apparent from the spelling. When it comes to pronunciation, pity the poor Spanish speaker who is trying to master English. How do you explain the pronunciation of *though, through, bough, thought, trough*, and *rough*? Six different pronunciations for the spelling *-ough*! (As more than one comedian has pointed out, you would expect no less from a language in which you drive on a parkway and park in a driveway, or in which you first cut a tree down and then you cut it up.) Be thankful that you are learning Spanish. With a few rules you are on your way.

Just one brief disclaimer: We are going to give you a guide to the pronunciation that is most widely used in Latin America. Naturally, there are variations in some parts of Latin America and in some parts of Spain. However, this pronunciation guide will give you a Spanish pronunciation that is recognizable and acceptable everywhere.

## VOWELS

All vowels have one sound each. All vowels, except for the occasionally silent *u*, make a sound. The sounds are these:

| Vowel | Pronunciation | Examples |
|---|---|---|
| a | ah | casa, calabaza |
| e | eh | mete, vete, leche |
| i | ee | dinero, insistí |
| o | oh | oso, mozo, pozo |
| u | oo | cucú |

Exceptions:

| | |
|---|---|
| 1) *U* is always silent after *q*. | que, queja, queso, química |
| 2) *U* is silent when it follows *g* and precedes *e* or *i*. | guerra, guía, guitarra |
| Exception to the exceptions: Putting two dots above a *u* changes a silent *u* into a *u* with an *oo* sound. | pingüino |

## CONSONANTS

Most Spanish consonants are very similar to their English counterparts.

| Consonant | Pronunciation | Examples |
|---|---|---|
| b | as in English though a tad softer, somewhere between *b* and *v* | barco, béisbol, bicicleta |
| c | as a *k* if it appears before *a, o, u,* or a consonant | casa, copa, cura, acto |
| | as an *s* if it appears before *e* or *i* | cero, cita |
| | Here is a word with both types of *c*. | acción |
| ch | as in the English word *chase* | charco, chispa, coche, muchacho |

| | | |
|---|---|---|
| d | quite a bit softer in Spanish than in English, somewhere between a *d* and a *th* in the English word *then* | dama, desde, dibujo |
| f | similar to English | foca |
| g | if it appears before *a*, *o*, or *u*, then as a *g* in the English word *gaff* | gafas, goma, gusano |
| | if it appears before *e* or *i*, then as an *h* in the English word *hat*, but with a slightly rough sound as if you were clearing your throat. | gente, gigante |
| | Note that a *u* that follows a *g* and precedes an *i* or an *e* is silent, so that *gue* in Spanish is pronounced as in the English guest and *gui* in Spanish is always pronounced as in the English geese. | guerra guitarra |
| h | always silent | hijo, hola |
| j | as an *h* in the English word *hat* though with a slight rough sound as if you were clearing your throat. | jirafa, jota |
| k | as in English | karate, kilo |
| l | as in English | lata, leche, listo, lomo, lujo |
| ll | as a *y* in the English word *yes* | llanta, llama, ella |
| m | as in English | mano, meta, mono |
| n | as in English | nada, ninguno, no |
| ñ | as the *ny* in the English word *canyon* | niño, cariño, caña |
| p | as in English, but slightly softer | papel, pecho, pino |
| qu | as a *k* | que, quemar, quitar |
| r | if it begins a word or follows a consonant, then with a roll of the tongue against the roof of the mouth, like the Spanish *rr* below; | raza, reto, risa, rosa |

| | | |
|---|---|---|
| | if between two vowels, then with a single flick of the tongue against the roof of the mouth near the teeth, closer to the Spanish *d* than the English *r* | eres, interesante, pero |
| rr | with a roll of the tongue against the roof of the mouth | perro, cigarro, burro |
| s | as in English | sapo, seta, sin, sopa |
| t | as in English, perhaps a bit less percussive | taco, techo, tinto, todo |
| v | as an English *b* though a tad softer, somewhere between English *b* and *v* (the Spanish *b* and *v* are identical) | vaca, ven, visita |
| w | sometimes, as a Spanish *v* (see above) and sometimes like the English *w*; mostly not used except for foreign words (which is why its pronunciation varies) | whiskey |
| x | if it begins a word, then like an *s* | xenofobia |
| | if within a word, then like the English *x* in exist | exige, existencia |
| | Exception: In many proper nouns (names of people and places) it is pronounced like a Spanish *j* | Ximena, México, Quixote |
| y | as in English | yate, yerno |
| z | same as the *s* | zorro |

## WHERE TO PUT THE STRESS

### If the Word Has No Written Accent

Some Spanish words are written with an accent, such as *ratón*. Most Spanish words do not have written accents, such as *rata*. For words without written accents, Spanish has two very simple rules for stressing syllables.

1) Words that end in a vowel, *n*, or *s* have the accent on the second to last syllable. This is the vast majority of words in Spanish.

| Word as written: | STRESS |
|---|---|
| rata (rat) | RA-ta |
| ventana (window) | ven-TA-na |
| lejos (far) | LE-jos |
| come (eat) | CO-me |

2) Words that end in a consonant (except *n* or *s*) have the stress on the last syllable.

| Word as written: | STRESS: |
|---|---|
| comer (to eat) | co-MER |
| tambor (drum) | tam-BOR |
| tener (to have) | te-NER |
| televisor (television set) | te-le-vi-SOR |

### When Vowels Are Found Together

When vowels are found together, such as the *ia* in the word *feria* and the *ea* in *gatea*, we need to know whether each letter is a separate syllable or whether the two vowels form one syllable, that is, a diphthong. Spanish handles this by dividing vowels into strong vowels and weak vowels:

Strong vowels: a, e, o
Weak vowels: i, u

Some remember this rule by reciting the sentence "You and I are weak." The rules for stressing double-vowel syllables are these:

1) If two *strong* vowels appear together, then each is treated as part of a separate syllable.

| Word as written: | STRESS: |
|---|---|
| gatea (crawl) | ga-TE-a |
| teatro (theatre) | te-A-tro |
| paseo (a walk) | pa-SE-o |
| leer (to read) | le-ER |
| crear (to create) | cre-AR |

2) If a weak vowel accompanies a strong vowel or two weak vowels appear together, the two vowels are treated as part of a single syllable, that is, as a diphthong.

The following are some of the more common diphthongs:

| Diphthong | Pronunciation | Example |
|---|---|---|
| ia | "ya" as in *yacht* | BEStia (beast) |
| ie | "ye" as in *yesterday* | pie (foot) |
| io | "yo" as in *yoyo* | camIÓN (truck) |
| ua | "wa" as in *water* | GUARdia (guard) |
| ue | "we" as in *wet* | CUEro (leather) |
| uo | "wo" as in *woe* | CUOta (quota) |
| ai | "i" as in *hi* | CAIgo (I fall) |
| ei | "ay" as in *play* | PLEIto (court case) |
| au | "ow" as in *cow* | GAUcho (Argentine cowboy) |
| ui | "wee" as in *weep* | BUItre (vulture) |

When applying the rules of stress, a diphthong is treated as a single syllable. Again, if the word ends in a vowel, *n*, or *s*, then the stress falls on the second to last syllable. Otherwise, the stress falls on the last syllable.

| Word: | STRESS: |
|---|---|
| importancia | im-por-TAN-cia (importance) |
| lenguas | LEN-guas (languages) |
| continuo | con-TI-nuo (continuous) |
| peine | PEI-ne (comb) |
| causa | CAU-sa (cause) |

### Words with Written Accents

Many Spanish words have written accents that indicate that the usual rules will not be followed. Written accents on multisyllable words have two effects:

1) They put the stress on the accented syllable.

2) In the case of two vowels found together, a written accent on a weak vowel changes it to a strong one. When this happens, a new syllable is created where before only a diphthong existed.

| Word as written: | STRESS: |
|---|---|
| ratón | ra-TON (mouse) |
| panadería | pa-na-de-RI-a (bakery) |
| leído | le-I-do (read) |
| tenía | te-NI-a (had) |
| ríe | RI-e (laughs) |

The above rules handle about 99 percent of the cases. There are a few special rules that we will not bore you with. Suffice it to say that you may occasionally come across a word that does not follow the above rules. At that point you will learn it. (We will indicate to you whenever such a word appears in this book.) Also, you will sometimes see one-syllable words with written accents. In this case, the accent does not affect the pronunciation of the word. Rather, it differentiates its meaning from the unaccented form of the same word (e.g., *más* = more; *mas* = but).

# GRAMMAR ENOUGH
# TO GET YOU STARTED

What follows is a set of preliminary grammar lessons. We provide them for those who are curious about why some things are said the way they are. You can use this section as a reference (and we do refer to it upon occasion in the phrasebook), or you may pick a lesson a day to bring yourself up to speed. There is a good deal of useful information here for those seeking to improve their Spanish in daily conversation with their kids, but this is not intended to be an exhaustive grammar review by any means. For example, we don't talk about the subjunctive mood, even though it is used quite often in Spanish. Understanding the subjunctive and its uses belongs to a more comprehensive study of grammar. In keeping with the goals of this book, we have tried to provide a broad and easy-to-follow outline that focuses on the most useful rules rather than the exceptions. Those who are interested in pursuing the language more in depth, however, should go to the "Spanish Language Resources" section for more materials. There you will find a list of books, CDs, and computer programs to help you with your studies.

## NUMBERS AND COUNTING

Lesson one is learning how to count. Here are the numbers:

| | | | | | | | |
|---|---|---|---|---|---|---|---|
| 0 | cero | 27 | veintisiete | 300 | trescientos | | |
| 1 | uno | 28 | veintiocho | 400 | cuartrocientos | | |
| 2 | dos | 29 | veintinueve | 500 | quinientos | | |
| 3 | tres | 30 | treinta | 600 | seiscientos | | |
| 4 | cuatro | 31 | treinta y uno | 700 | setecientos | | |
| 5 | cinco | 32 | treinta y dos | 800 | ochocientos | | |
| 6 | seis | | | 900 | novecientos | | |
| 7 | siete | 40 | cuarenta | | | | |
| 8 | ocho | 41 | cuarenta y uno | 1,000 | mil | | |
| 9 | nueve | 42 | cuarenta y dos | 1,001 | mil y uno | | |
| 10 | diez | | | 1,002 | mil dos | | |
| 11 | once | 50 | cincuenta | 1,003 | mil tres | | |
| 12 | doce | 51 | cincuenta y uno | 1,057 | mil cincuenta y siete | | |
| 13 | trece | 52 | cincuenta y dos | 1,345 | mil trescientos cuarenta y cinco | | |
| 14 | catorce | | | | | | |
| 15 | quince | 60 | sesenta | 2,000 | dos mil | | |
| 16 | dieciséis | 70 | setenta | 2,001 | dos mil uno | | |
| 17 | diecisiete | 80 | ochenta | 2,034 | dos mil treinta y cuatro | | |
| 18 | dieciocho | 90 | noventa | | | | |
| 19 | diecinueve | | | 3,000 | tres mil | | |
| 20 | veinte | 100 | ciento (cien) | 4,000 | cuatro mil | | |
| 21 | veintiuno | 101 | ciento uno | 10,000 | diez mil | | |
| 22 | veintidós | 102 | ciento dos | 25,000 | veinticinco mil | | |
| 23 | veintitrés | | | 100,000 | cien mil | | |
| 24 | veinticuatro | 200 | doscientos | 200,000 | doscientos mil | | |
| 25 | veinticinco | 201 | doscientos uno | 1,000,000 | un millón | | |
| 26 | veintiséis | 202 | doscientos dos | 100,000,000 | cien millones | | |
| | | | | 200,000,000 | doscientos millones | | |

It is interesting to note that what is called a billion in U.S. English—the number 1,000,000,000—was known as a thousand million (or a *milliard*) in England until 1974. The word *billion* was used to denote the number 1,000,000,000,000. In Spanish *un billón* refers to this latter number. Our billion in Spanish is *mil millones,* literally a thousand million.

Notes:

1. *Ciento,* when used as an adjective or when it multiplies the next number, becomes *cien. Uno* becomes *un* when it modifies a masculine noun and *una* when it modifies a feminine noun.

> *cien mil gatos* (a hundred thousand cats) [multiplies one thousand]
> *cien gatos* (a hundred cats) [used as an adjective]
> *ciento cincuenta gatos* (a hundred fifty cats) [does not multiply the next number]
> *un gato* (one cat, a cat)

2. *Mil y uno* can also be written *mil uno.* Numbers after this (*mil dos, mil tres*, etc.), do not use *y*.

3. *Uno* and *cientos* are the only two numbers that change to agree in gender with the nouns they modify. (Note that *cien* and *ciento* do not change when they are used as adjectives.)

> *una guitarra* (one guitar, a guitar)
> *ciento un gatos* (101 cats)
> *ciento una guitarras* (101 guitars)
> *cuatrocientos gatos* (400 cats)
> *cuatrocientas guitarras* (400 guitars)
> *mil cuatrocientas cincuenta y una guitarras* (1,451 guitars)

4. The number *millón* requires a *de* when modifying a noun.

> *tres millones de gatos* (3 million cats)

5. Numbers are masculine. However, when they replace or refer to another noun they take on the gender of the noun.

> *el cinco de espadas* (the five of spades)
> *Escribe un tres aquí.* (Write a three here.)
> *Entre las dos habitaciones, prefiero la dieciséis.* (Between the two rooms, I prefer number 16.) [*La dieciséis* refers to *la habitación dieciséis.*]

6. Note the following expressions and patterns for doing simple math:

> *dos y tres son cinco* (two and three is five)
> *tres menos uno son dos* (three minus one is two)
> *dos por tres son seis* (two times three is six)
> *diez dividido por dos son cinco* (ten divided by two is five)

**Ordinal numbers**

| | | | |
|---|---|---|---|
| first | *primero* | sixth | *sexto* |
| second | *segundo* | seventh | *séptimo* |
| third | *tercero* | eighth | *octavo* |
| fourth | *cuarto* | ninth | *noveno* |
| fifth | *quinto* | tenth | *décimo* |

Notes:

1. All of these must agree in gender with the nouns they modify:

*la quinta mujer* (the fifth woman)
*la segunda persona* (the second person)
*el octavo piso* (the eighth floor)

2. The masculine forms of *primero* and *tercero* drop the *-o* when used in front of nouns they modify. (The others do not.)

*el tercer piso* (the third floor)
*la tercera puerta* (the third door)
*el séptimo piso* (the seventh floor)

3. Even Spanish speakers have trouble remembering the ordinal numbers above ten and quite often use cardinal numbers instead.

*el aniversario treinta* (the thirtieth anniversary)
*el cliente dos mil* (the two-thousandth customer)

## NOUNS

### The gender of nouns

Nouns in Spanish are either masculine or feminine. Masculine nouns require masculine articles and masculine adjectives. Feminine nouns require feminine articles and feminine adjectives. Therefore, it is important to know the gender of a noun. Here are some clues to noun gender:

#### CLUES TO MASCULINE NOUNS

1. If a noun ends in an *o*, it is quite likely to be masculine.

   *el amigo* (male friend)

There are some exceptions, including *la mano* (the hand), and a few professions that can be either masculine or feminine:

| | |
|---|---|
| *el modelo* (male model) | *la modelo* (female model) |
| *el piloto* (male pilot) | *la piloto* (female pilot) |
| *el soldado* (male soldier) | *la soldado* (female soldier) |

2. If a noun ends in an *or*, it is likely to be masculine.

   *el calor* (heat)
   *el amor* (love)

3. If a noun ends in *-aje*, it is likely to be masculine.

   *el equipaje* (luggage)

4. If a noun ends in a stressed (written accent) vowel, it is likely to be masculine.

   *el sofá* (sofa)
   *el champú* (shampoo)

CLUES TO FEMININE NOUNS

1. If a noun ends in an *a*, it is usually feminine.

*la amiga* (female friend)

However, there are a number of exceptions:
a. Greek-derived nouns ending in -*ma* are usually masculine, such as:

*el problema* (problem)
*el sistema* (system)
*el dilema* (dilemma)
*el poema* (poem)

But note that there are plenty of nouns that end in -*ma* that are feminine:

*la cama* (bed)
*la broma* (joke)
*la crema* (cream)
*la rama* (branch).

b. Some nouns always end in *a* and can be either masculine or feminine.

*el artista* (male artist)          *la artista* (female artist)
*el astronauta* (male astronaut)    *la astronauta* (female astronaut)
*el colega* (male colleague)        *la colega* (female colleague)

2. If a noun ends in -*ión*, it is usually feminine.

*la acción* (action)
*la decisión* (decision)

There are a couple of common exceptions here as well: *el avión* (airplane) and *el camión* (truck).

3. If a noun ends in -*dad*, -*tad*, or -*tud*, it is usually feminine:

*la verdad* (truth)
*la libertad* (liberty)

Of course, there are lots of nouns that do not fit into any of the above categories. You'll just have to learn these individually. In the phrase book and glossary, we indicate gender by including the article: *el gato, la cama*.

## The plural of nouns

As in English, the most common ways to form plurals in Spanish are:
1. If the noun ends in a vowel, add an -*s*:

*manos* (hands)
*mesas* (tables)
*casas* (houses)
*huevos* (eggs)

2. If the noun ends in a consonant, add an -*es*:

*relojes* (watches)
*colores* (colors)
*aviones* (airplanes)

Naturally, there are exceptions to these rules. (For example, nouns ending in -*á*, *í*, or *ú* take an -*es*.) However, the above two rules will cover the vast majority of cases.

## The gender of plural nouns

A group of boys is *niños*.
A group of girls is *niñas*.
A group of boys and girls is *niños*.

Thus mixed-gender groups are grammatically masculine. Consider:

*mi padre* (my father)
*mi madre* (my mother)
*mis padres* (my parents)
*mi tío* (my aunt)
*mi tía* (my uncle)
*mis tíos* (my aunts and uncles, or just my uncles, depending on the context)

## ADJECTIVES

Adjectives must agree with the nouns they modify, both in number and in gender. Let us look at articles first, and then at other adjectives.

### DEFINITE ARTICLES

|          | Masculine  | Feminine  |
|----------|-----------|-----------|
| **Singular** | el (the)  | la (the)  |
| **Plural**   | los (the) | las (the) |

*el reloj* (the watch)
*la casa* (the house)
*los relojes* (the watches)
*las casas* (the houses)

### INDEFINITE ARTICLES

|          | Masculine   | Feminine    |
|----------|-------------|-------------|
| **Singular** | un (a, an)  | una (a, an) |
| **Plural**   | unos (some) | unas (some) |

*un reloj* (a watch)
*una casa* (a house)
*unos relojes* (some watches)
*unas casas* (some houses)

### OTHER ADJECTIVES

Most other adjectives follow this same pattern, that is, they must agree in number and gender:

|          | Masculine    | Feminine    |
|----------|--------------|-------------|
| **Singular** | alto (tall)  | alta (tall) |
| **Plural**   | altos (tall) | altas (tall)|

*un hombre alto* (a tall man)
*una mujer alta* (a tall woman)
*unos hombres altos* (some tall men)
*unas mujeres altas* (some tall women)

Some adjectives do not have separate masculine and feminine forms:

|  | Masculine or Feminine |
|---|---|
| Singular | importante (important) |
| Plural | importantes (important) |

*un asunto importante* (an important issue)
*una película importante* (an important movie)
*unos asuntos importantes* (some important issues)
*unas películas importantes* (some important movies)

### INVARIABLE ADJECTIVES

It turns out that there are some adjectives that are invariable; they do not change for either number or gender. Some colors (*rosa, violeta, naranja*) are like this (see "Colors" section in this grammar guide). In addition, there are a few other adjectives that do not vary by number or gender:

| | |
|---|---|
| *macho* (male) | *una rata macho* (a male rat) |
| *hembra* (female) | *unos ratones hembra* (some female mice) |
| *encinta* (pregnant) | *cuatro mujeres encinta* (four pregnant women) |
| *modelo* (model) | *unas ciudades modelo* (some model cities) |
| *alerta* (alerta) | *un niño alerta* (an alert boy) |

### Position of adjectives

As a general rule, adjectives follow the nouns that they modify:

*la casa verde* (the green house)
*el hombre alto* (the tall man)

You will sometimes see an adjective in front of a noun. Typically, when this is done, it is to convey some emotional or dramatic feeling:

*una magnífica casa* (a magnificent house)
*un inquietante problema* (a troubling problem)

It would be fine to write these with the adjective after the noun, but putting it before the noun adds some emphasis.

There are some adjectives that change meaning depending on where you put them, before or after. Often putting the adjective before makes it more subjective, less literal.

*un hombre grande* (a big man)
*un gran hombre* (a great man)
*un niño pobre* (a poor boy, that is, not rich)
*un pobre niño* (a poor boy, that is, unfortunate)

The bottom line is that you are usually going to put the adjectives after the noun. Through experience, you will gradually get a feel for when it is appropriate to put the adjective in front of the noun.

## COLORS

Here are some common colors:

*rojo* (red)
*anaranjado, naranja* (orange)
*amarillo* (yellow)
*verde* (green)
*azul* (blue)
*morado* (purple)
*violeta* (violet)
*blanco* (white)
*negro* (black)
*rosado, rosa* (pink)
*café* (brown)
*marrón* (brown)

Colors are most often used as adjectives and thus, like other adjectives, agree both in number and in gender with the nouns they are modifying.

|  | Masculine | Feminine |
|---|---|---|
| Singular | rojo (red) | roja (red) |
| Plural | rojos (red) | rojas (red) |

However, some colors vary just by number:

|  | Masculine or Feminine |
|---|---|
| Singular | verde (green) |
| Plural | verdes (green) |

And some colors do not vary at all. These colors are really nouns being used as adjectives. For example:

*Rosa* (pink) is just the name of the flower.
*Violeta* (violet) is just the name of the flower.
*Naranja* (orange) is just the name of the fruit.
*Café* (coffee-colored) is just coffee.
*Oro* (gold) is just the name of the mineral.

Thus we have:

> *el coche naranja* (the orange car)
> *los pantalones rosa* (the pink pants)
> *el teléfono violeta* (the violet telephone)

Notes:

1. There are two ways to say orange: *anaranjado* (which varies according to number and gender) and *naranja* (which is invariable). Likewise, there are two different ways to say pink: *rosado* (which varies according to number and gender) and *rosa* (which is invariable).

2. There are some writers who will pluralize so-called invariable color adjectives (*los pantalones rosas*), and this is becoming more acceptable. However, they never change the gender (never *los pantalones rosos*).

3. All compound colors are invariable:

> *una mesa rojo oscuro* (a dark red table)
> *unos ojos azul pálido* (pale blue eyes)

## POSSESSIVES

### Possessive adjectives

Possessive adjectives show possession or connection. In English these are words such as *my, your, his, her, its*, and *their*. In Spanish, possessive adjectives, like other adjectives, must agree in number and (sometimes) gender with the nouns they are modifying. Here they are:

|  | Masculine Singular | Feminine Singular | Masculine Plural | Feminine Plural |
|---|---|---|---|---|
| **my** | mi | mi | mis | mis |
| **your (familiar)** | tu | tu | tus | tus |
| **his, hers, its your (formal)** | su | su | sus | sus |
| **our** | nuestro | nuestra | nuestros | nuestras |
| **their your (plural)** | su | su | sus | sus |

*mi perro* (my dog)

*nuestra casa* (our house)

*tu mesa* (your table—informal directed at one person)

These possessive adjectives go in front of the noun, as in the above examples. Occasionally, possessive adjectives can go after the noun. In such cases, with the exception of the Spanish form for the English *our*, however, they have a different longer form:

|  | Masculine Singular | Feminine Singular | Masculine Plural | Feminine Plural |
|---|---|---|---|---|
| **my** | mío | mía | míos | mías |
| **your (familiar)** | tuyo | tuya | tuyos | tuyas |
| **his, hers, its your (formal)** | suyo | suya | suyos | suyas |
| **our** | nuestro | nuestra | nuestros | nuestras |
| **their your (plural)** | suyo | suya | suyos | suyas |

*la cama mía* (my bed)
*un amigo mío* (a friend of mine)


### Possessive pronouns

The longer forms of the possessive adjectives (*mío, tuyo*, etc.) may also be used as possessive pronouns:

*Es mío* (It is mine.)
*El nuestro es muy caro.* (Ours is very expensive.)

Note: When the possessive pronoun follows the verb *ser* and is used to show possession, you will usually omit the article, as in the first sentence above. Otherwise, you should use the article as in the second sentence above. Again, with experience, you will begin to get a feel for this.

## DEMONSTRATIVES

### Demonstrative adjectives

In English demonstrative adjectives are *this* and *that* and their plurals, *these* and *those*. Spanish has more: *este*, *ese*, and *aquel* and their plurals. Spanish demonstratives also change according to gender:

|  | Masculine Singular | Feminine Singular | Masculine Plural | Feminine Plural |
|---|---|---|---|---|
| **this** | este | esta | estos | estas |
| **that** | ese | esa | esos | esas |
| **that** | aquel | aquella | aquellos | aquellas |

For English speakers, the problem is when to use *ese* and its variations and when to use *aquel* and its variations, all of which mean *that*. In general, *aquel* is further away in space or in time. Here are a few simple rules:

1. When in doubt, use *ese*.

2. *Aquel* can be used for differentiating between to two things that are far away. For example:

*¿Ese coche o aquel coche?* (That car or that car over there?)

### Demonstrative pronouns

All of the above demonstrative adjectives can be used as pronouns, that is, they can stand alone, serving as nouns:

*¿Qué coche? Ese.* (Which car? That one.)

Note that some writers distinguish the pronoun from the adjective by putting a written accent on the pronoun: *ése* for the pronoun, and *ese* for the adjective. Modern usage, however, permits both of them without the written accent.

### Neuter demonstrative pronouns

In Spanish there exist three demonstrative pronouns that do not have a gender: *esto*, *eso*, and *aquello*. These are used to refer to things either without a gender (such as ideas) or whose gender is unknown:

> *¿Qué es eso?* (What is that?) [gender unknown]
> *No quiero hablar de eso.* (I don't want to talk about that.) [referring to an idea, concept, or matter]

## COMPARATIVES AND SUPERLATIVES

### Comparing quantities of nouns

There are several ways to compare nouns. If you are talking about quantities of things, you would use the following expressions:

more: *más . . . que*
less: *menos . . . que*
same: *tanto (tanta, tantos, tantas) . . . como*

*Este libro tiene más páginas que ese libro.* (This book as more pages than that book has.)
*Tienes tantos juguetes como ella.* (You have as many toys as she has.)

In the above expressions, *más, menos, tanto (tanta, tantos, tantas)* are adjectives. Like most adjectives, these can be turned into nouns.

*Yo tengo más que tú.* (I have more than you.)

In the case of *tanto, tanta, tantos, tantas*, the forms chosen must have the same number and gender as the nouns they are referring to. For example, if you were referring to toys (*juguetes*), you might say:

*Saraí tiene tantos que su hermana.* (Saraí has as many as her sister.)

Note that in front of numbers, *más . . . que* and *menos . . . que* become *más . . . de* and *menos . . . de.*

*Yo tengo más de cuatro coches.* (I have more than four cars.)

### Comparing qualities of nouns

If you want to compare the qualities of a noun, then you will use the following expressions in conjunction with an adjective.

more: *más . . . que*
less: *menos . . . que*
same: *tan . . . como*

*Roberto es más alto que yo.* (Robert is taller than I.)
*Juan es más pequeño que Pablo.* (John is smaller than Paul.)
*Este asunto es menos importante que ese.* (This matter is less important than that one.)
*Jenny es tan alta como María.* (Jenny is as tall as Mary.)
*Sus hijas son tan altas como él.* (His daughters are as tall as he is.)

Technically, *más, menos,* and *tan,* as used above, are adverbs that are modifying adjectives. As always, the adjectives must agree in number and gender with the noun they are modifying. As in English, a few words have special comparative adjectives:

| | |
|---|---|
| *bueno* (good) | *mejor* (better) |
| *malo* (bad) | *peor* (worse) |
| *grande* (big) | *mayor* (bigger) |
| *viejo* (old) | *mayor* (older) |
| *joven* (young) | *menor* (younger) |

*Este vino es mejor que ése.* (This wine is better than that one.)

Note: Sometimes one uses *mayor* for 'bigger,' and sometimes one uses *más grande.* (And sometimes one can use either.) You shouldn't worry about this subtlety now. As you learn phrases you will get a feel of which to use. (If you are really curious, you can consult one of the grammar books we recommend.) When you want to say "older" and are referring to people, however, *mayor* is a better choice than *más viejo.*

Note: You can qualify *más* and *menos* with *mucho* and *poco* as in:

*Roberto es mucho más alto que yo.* (Robert is much taller than I.)
*Tengo muchas más manzanas que tú.* (I have many more apples than you.)

(If *mucho* and *poco* are used as adjectives, as in the second sentence above, they must agree with the noun in number and gender.)

### Comparing actions

Comparative adverbs can also be used to compare actions, that is, to modify verbs. The following adverbs can be applied directly to verbs:

more: *más . . . que*
less: *menos . . . que*
same: *tanto . . . como*

*Pepe habla tanto como yo.* (Pepe speaks as much as I do.)
*Leo más que mi hermana.* (I read more than my sister does.)

The following adverbs can be combined with other adverbs:

more: *más . . . que*
less: *menos . . . que*
same: *tan . . . como*

*Elena habla tan rápido como yo.* (Elena speaks as rapidly as I do.)

Again, a few words have special comparatives:

| | |
|---|---|
| *mal* (badly) | *peor* (worse) |
| *bien* (well) | *mejor* (better) |

*Lo hizo mejor que yo.* (He did it better than I did.)

### Superlatives

Often an article (*el, la, los, las*) or possessive (*mi, tu, su,* etc.) is used to form the superlative of an adjective:

*el libro más importante de todos* (the most important book of all)
*mi amigo más íntimo* (my closest friend)
*la casa más grande del barrio* (the biggest house in the neighborhood)

There are other constructions and situations in which the article or possessive can be (or should be) omitted. (Again, if you are interested in these finer points, check out one of the grammar books we recommend.)

The superlative of an adverb is formed as follows:

*De todos los coches, éste va más rápido.* (Of all the cars, this one goes fastest.)

## PERSONAL PRONOUNS (AND THE PERSONAL *A*)

There is considerable variation in the Spanish-speaking world regarding the use of personal pronouns, especially direct and indirect objects. The following table shows the most common usage in Latin America. However, as you progress and start reading you will begin to notice the variations.

| | | Subject | Direct Object | Indirect Object | Object of a Preposition |
|---|---|---|---|---|---|
| **Singular** | | | | | |
| **1st Person** | I, me | yo | me | me | mí |
| **2nd Person** | you<br>you | tú (familiar)<br>usted (formal) | te<br>lo, la | te<br>le | ti<br>usted |
| **3rd Person** | he, him, it<br>she, her, it | él<br>ella | lo<br>la | le<br>le | él<br>ella |
| **Plural** | | | | | |
| **1st Person** | we, us<br>we, us | nosotros<br>nosotras | nos<br>nos | nos<br>nos | nosotros<br>nosotras |
| **2nd Person** | you, you | ustedes | los, las | les | ustedes |
| **3rd Person** | they, them<br>they, them | ellos<br>ellas | los<br>las | les<br>les | ellos<br>ellas |

### Subject pronouns

Because verbs in Spanish are almost fully conjugated, one can usually determine the subject from the verb form. Therefore, subject pronouns are usually omitted:

*Hablo español.* (I speak Spanish.)
*Vamos al cine.* (We are going to the movies.)

Although, strictly speaking, it is not grammatically incorrect to use the subject pronoun, its overuse simply sounds nonnative. You should strive to use it only where necessary to avoid ambiguity or confusion. For example, if you have been speaking about more than one person and need to be clear about which you are referring to:

*Él habla constantemente.* (He talks constantly. [Not she.])

You may also use a subject pronoun for emphasis:

*Yo hablo español.* (*I* speak Spanish. [But you don't.])

### Object pronouns

To briefly review our basic grammar, object pronouns replace nouns that are the objects of verbs. Direct objects receive the action of the verb directly, while indirect objects usually indicate to whom or for whom an action is being done. Typically, object pronouns go before the conjugated verb.

*Te quiero.* (I love you.)
*Me gusta este carro.* (I like this car. Literally, this car pleases me.)
*¿Me puedes dar el libro?* (Can you give me the book?)

As an option, object pronouns can be attached to an infinitive or present participle.

*¿Puedes darme el libro?* (Can you give me the book?)
*Te estoy esperando.* (I am waiting for you.)
*Estoy esperándote.* (I am waiting for you.)

In an affirmative command (that is, when you are telling someone to do something), the object pronoun *must* be attached to the verb.

*Dame el libro.* (Give me the book.)
*Espérame.* (Wait for me.)

Note that negative commands follow the general rule of placing the object pronouns before the verb.

*No me des el libro.* (Don't give me the book.)
*No me esperes.* (Don't wait for me.)

If the options mentioned above are a bit confusing, just remember that object pronouns can always go before the conjugated verb, with the only necessary exception being affirmative commands.

### MORE THAN ONE PRONOUN

As in English, you may use more than one pronoun at a time (Give me it.) Here are a couple of rules that *almost* always work (don't worry about the exceptions!):

1. The indirect object pronoun comes before the direct object pronoun.

*¿Quieres dármelo?* (Will you give it to me?)
*Te lo compré.* (I bought you it. [I bought it for you.])

2. When there is an indirect object pronoun in the third person (*le* or *les*) in conjunction with the direct object pronoun in the third person (*lo, la, los,* or *las*), Spanish avoids the double *l*. Change the indirect object pronoun to *se*.

*Cuando veas a Ana, ¿quieres dárselo?* (When you see Ana, will you give it to her?)
*Ese libro es de mis hermanos. Se lo compré.* (That book is my brothers'. I bought it for them.)

Again, do this only where there is both an indirect and a direct object pronoun in the third person:

*¿Quieres darle el libro?* (Will you give him the book?)
*¿Quieres dárselo?* (Will you give it to him?)

There are rare occasions when this rule will not work, although it may be years before you see an exception.

Note: Oftentimes a noun indirect object will be preceded (redundantly) by an indirect object pronoun:

*Le doy la bicicleta a Juana.* (I am giving the bicycle to Jane.)

In the above sentence the *le* is redundant (because it refers to Juana, who is also named in the sentence) but is usually required. Typically there is no redundancy for the direct object pronoun.

Note: Pronominal (reflexive) verbs almost always have the reflexive pronoun first, followed by the object pronoun:

*Se me olvidó.* (I forgot it. [Literally, it forgot itself to me.])
*Se le olvidó.* (He forgot it. [Literally, it forgot itself to him.])

### Prepositional pronouns

Most prepositions take prepositional pronouns. They are *mí, ti, él, ella, usted, nosotros, ellos, ellas, ustedes.* Note that these are the same as the subject pronouns except in the first- and second-person singular.

*Voy con él.* (I am going with him.)
*No sabes nada de mí.* (You don't know anything about me.)

The preposition *con* when combined with *mí* or *ti* results in the words *conmigo* and *contigo.*

*Voy contigo.* (I am going with you.)
*¿Quieres venir conmigo?* (Do you want to come with me?)

Note: The preposition *entre* (among or between) and *según* (according to) typically take subject pronouns.

*Según tú, el asunto no es importante.* (According to you, the matter is not important.)
*No hay nada entre tú y yo.* (There is nothing between you and me.)

Note: Other prepositions, such as *excepto* (except), *hasta* (even), *incluso* (including), and *salvo* (except) can take a subject pronoun if they refer to subjects.

*Hasta yo puedo hacerlo.* (Even I can do it.)
*Todos van, salvo tú.* (Everyone is going, except you.)

### The personal *a*

It is important to understand that when a direct object is a person, it is preceded by the "personal *a.*"

*Vimos la taza.* (We saw the cup.)
*Vimos a María.* (We saw María.)
*Llevé a mis amigos a la fiesta.* (I took my friends to the party.)

There are some exceptions to this rule. For example, if you are not referring to someone in particular, you will omit the personal *a*.

*Busco un médico.* (I am looking for a doctor.)
*Busco al médico.* (I am looking for the doctor.)

In the first sentence, I am not looking for any particular doctor. In the second sentence, I have a particular doctor in mind.

As for animals, pets almost always take the personal *a*:

*Quiero pasear al perro.* (I want to walk the dog.)
*Llevé al gato a mi casa.* (I took the cat to my house.)

Other animals do not take the personal *a*, unless the speaker wants to humanize them in some way (as in many children's stories).

Pronouns that represent people usually take the personal *a*. This includes the pronoun *nadie*.

*No tengo a nadie.* (I don't have anyone.)
*Vi a alguien en la calle.* (I saw someone in the street.)
*¿A quién buscas?* (For whom are you looking? Whom are you looking for?)

Note the following little wrinkles:
1. *Querer* without the personal *a* means *to want*; *querer* with the personal *a* means *to love*.

*Quiere un colega.* (She wants a colleague. She wants to have a colleague.)
*Quiere a un colega.* (She loves a colleague. She is in love with a colleague.)

2. *Tener* usually does not take the personal *a*. When it does it means something like *to consider, to take for,* or *to make*.

*Tiene dos hijos.* (He has two children.)
*Tiene a sus hijos por tontos.* (He takes his children for fools.)

## REGULAR VERBS

In this section we outline how regular verbs are conjugated in the present, simple past, the imperfect past, and the future. Other conjugations are treated in other sections. First, note the following:

1. There are two ways of saying *you* (singular): a formal, polite way and a familiar way. The subject pronoun for the familiar way is *tú*, and the verb form is that for the second person singular. The subject for the formal way is *usted*, which, oddly enough, takes the third person singular verb form. (This is because the subject pronoun for the formal way comes from *vuestra merced* [your mercy], which was once used in talking to the king.) So one says *usted habla* (you speak) to be polite and *tú hablas* (you speak) to be familiar.

2. For the plural form of you, Latin Americans say *ustedes hablan* (you all speak), again in the third person. In Latin America there is no separate formal and familiar form in the plural. (There is in Spain, but we are not going to consider it here.)

3. In Spanish there are three types of verbs, those ending in *-ar, -er,* and *-ir.*

### The present tense

|  | Subject Pronoun | hablar | comer | vivir |
|---|---|---|---|---|
| 1st person singular | yo (I) | habl-o | com-o | viv-o |
| 2nd person singular | tú (you—familiar) | habl-as | com-es | viv-es |
| 3rd person singular | él, ella (he, she) usted (you—formal) | habl-a | com-e | viv-e |
| 1st person plural | nosotros (we) nosotras (we) | habl-amos | com-emos | viv-imos |
| 3rd person plural | ellos, ellas (they) ustedes (you all) | habl-an | com-en | viv-en |

For many situations, the present tense is used much as it is in English.

*Habla mucho.* (He talks a lot.)
*Vivimos aquí.* (We live here.)

In some cases, the present tense can be used where in English a continuous form would be used.

*¿Qué haces?* (What are you doing?)

(Spanish also has continuous forms, which are covered in their own section of this grammar guide.)

### The preterite (simple past) tense (regular)

|  | Subject Pronoun | hablar | comer | vivir |
|---|---|---|---|---|
| 1st person singular | yo (I) | habl-é | com-í | viv-í |
| 2nd person singular | tú (you—familiar) | habl-aste | com-iste | viv-iste |
| 3rd person singular | él, ella (he, she) usted (you—formal) | habl-ó | com-ió | viv-ió |
| 1st person plural | nosotros (we) nosotras (we) | habl-amos | com-imos | viv-imos |
| 3rd person plural | ellos, ellas (they) ustedes (you all) | habl-aron | com-ieron | viv-ieron |

The simple past (also known as the preterite) is generally used to narrate singular events in the past that are viewed as completed, that is, not ongoing or routine. More on this when we contrast the preterite and imperfect tenses below.

*Cantaron ayer.* (They sang yesterday.)
*Hablé con tu maestra.* (I spoke with your teacher.)

## The imperfect past tense

|  | Subject Pronoun | hablar | comer | vivir |
|---|---|---|---|---|
| **1st person singular** | yo (I) | habl-aba | com-ía | viv-ía |
| **2nd person singular** | tú (you—familiar) | habl-abas | com-ías | viv-ías |
| **3rd person singular** | él, ella (he, she) usted (you—formal) | habl-aba | com-ía | viv-ía |
| **1st person plural** | nosotros (we) nosotras (we) | habl-ábamos | com-íamos | viv-íamos |
| **3rd person plural** | ellos, ellas (they) ustedes (you all) | habl-aban | com-ían | viv-ían |

The imperfect past is used for events or states that are perceived as routine or as going on for a period in the past.

The imperfect is often translated into English using a past continuous form.

> *Hablábamos mientras los niños jugaban.* (We were talking while the children were playing.)

It can also have the meaning of "used to," connoting routine in the past.

> *Cuando era niño, Beto iba al parque mucho.* (When he was a boy, Beto went [used to go] to the park a lot.)

Many of the most common verbs in Spanish have irregular conjugations. (This is true in English as well.) In this section we give the conjugations of some of the most important of these verbs (in alphabetical order) in the tenses you will need most often: the present, the simple past (also called the preterite), the imperfect, and the future. Whereas the usage of the present and future tenses differ only in minor ways from their counterparts in English, and therefore present few difficulties, the rules dictating the usage of the simple past and the imperfect are more involved. This book is not intended as a complete grammar guide, so we will not provide a full account here (any grammar book will explain this, and a web search with the key words *preterite, imperfect,* and *Spanish* will yield abundant free materials), but the following very abbreviated explanation may hold you for now.

## THE SIMPLE PAST (PRETERITE) AND THE IMPERFECT CONTRASTED

The simple past is used to tell of events that move the narrative forward in a sequence of actions.

*Me levanté a las siete, desayuné y fui a trabajar.* (I got up at seven, had breakfast, and went to work.)

The imperfect, on the other hand, is used to describe the scene, tell about ongoing states or actions, or to talk about actions that were repeated in the past (what *used to* happen, as mentioned above).

*Hacía sol y María leía en el banco del parque como hacía cuando era niña.*
(It was sunny and Maria was reading on the park bench, like she used to do when she was a little girl.)

Of course, we usually alternate between these tenses when we talk about the past.

*Llovía esa mañana cuando Pedro se levantó. Por la ventana vio un carro que iba por la calle. Era un carro viejo como tenía su padre cuando vivían en California.* (It was raining that morning when Pedro got up. Through the window he saw a car going down the street. It was an old car like his father used to have when they lived in California.)

Often an ongoing imperfect action will be interrupted by a simple past action.

*Antonio leía cuando Sara llamó a la puerta.* (Antonio was reading when Sara knocked on the door.)

In the above example, the action of reading was going on when another action, knocking, happened. Thus reading is in the imperfect tense and knocking is in the simple past (or preterite). You can see that the choice between the simple past and the imperfect past reflects the meaning you want to convey. If you want to convey the idea that the action was ongoing or routine, use the imperfect.

## The future tense (regular)

|  | Subject Pronoun | hablar | comer | vivir |
|---|---|---|---|---|
| 1st person singular | yo (I) | hablar-é | comer-é | vivir-é |
| 2nd person singular | tú (you—familiar) | hablar-ás | comer-ás | vivir-ás |
| 3rd person singular | él, ella (he, she) usted (you—formal) | hablar-á | comer-á | vivir-á |
| 1st person plural | nosotros (we) nosotras (we) | hablar-emos | comer-emos | vivir-emos |
| 3rd person plural | ellos, ellas (they) ustedes (you all) | hablar-án | comer-án | vivir-án |

The future is not used as much in Spanish as it is in English. Oftentimes a Spanish speaker will use a form of *ir a* (to go to) in order to convey a future action.

> *Voy a hablar con tu maestra mañana.* (I am going to speak with your teacher tomorrow.)

instead of

> *Hablaré con tu maestro mañana.* (I will speak with your teacher tomorrow.)

In this book, most of the references to the future will use the *ir a* construction rather than the future tense.

## IRREGULAR VERBS

Many of the most common verbs in Spanish have irregular conjugations. (This is true in English as well.) In this section we give the conjugations of some of the most important of these verbs. Certainly a verb may have irregular forms in one tense and not in another. The imperfect tense only has three irregular verbs, *ir* (to go), *ser* (to be), and *ver* (to see). Still, we give the forms for each verb in all four tenses, whether they are irregular or not, for the sake of convenience. These are listed in alphabetical order. (The conjugations for *estar* and *ser* can be found in the "To Be or Not To Be" section, and *haber* is covered under "Compound Tenses" below.

### *Dar* (To give)

| | Subject Pronoun | Present | Simple Past | Imperfect | Future |
|---|---|---|---|---|---|
| 1st person singular | yo (I) | doy | di | daba | daré |
| 2nd person singular | tú (you—familiar) | das | diste | dabas | darás |
| 3rd person singular | él, ella (he, she) usted (you—formal) | da | dio | daba | dará |
| 1st person plural | nosotros (we) nosotras (we) | damos | dimos | dábamos | daremos |
| 3rd person plural | ellos, ellas (they) ustedes (you all) | dan | dieron | daban | darán |

## *Decir* (To give)

|  | Subject Pronoun | Present | Simple Past | Imperfect | Future |
|---|---|---|---|---|---|
| 1st person singular | yo (I) | digo | dije | decía | diré |
| 2nd person singular | tú (you—familiar) | dices | dijiste | decías | dirás |
| 3rd person singular | él, ella (he, she) usted (you—formal) | dice | dijo | decía | dirá |
| 1st person plural | nosotros (we) nosotras (we) | decimos | dijimos | decíamos | diremos |
| 3rd person plural | ellos, ellas (they) ustedes (you all) | dicen | dijeron | decían | dirán |

## *Hacer* (To do, to make)

|  | Subject Pronoun | Present | Simple Past | Imperfect | Future |
|---|---|---|---|---|---|
| 1st person singular | yo (I) | hago | hice | hacía | haré |
| 2nd person singular | tú (you—familiar) | haces | hiciste | hacías | harás |
| 3rd person singular | él, ella (he, she) usted (you—formal) | hace | hizo | hacía | hará |
| 1st person plural | nosotros (we) nosotras (we) | hacemos | hicimos | hacíamos | haremos |
| 3rd person plural | ellos, ellas (they) ustedes (you all) | hacen | hicieron | hacían | harán |

### *Ir* (To go)

| | Subject Pronoun | Present | Simple Past | Imperfect | Future |
|---|---|---|---|---|---|
| 1st person singular | yo (I) | voy | fui | iba | iré |
| 2nd person singular | tú (you—familiar) | vas | fuiste | ibas | irás |
| 3rd person singular | él, ella (he, she) usted (you—formal) | va | fue | iba | irá |
| 1st person plural | nosotros (we) nosotras (we) | vamos | fuimos | íbamos | iremos |
| 3rd person plural | ellos, ellas (they) ustedes (you all) | van | fueron | iban | irán |

### *Poder* (To be able)

| | Subject Pronoun | Present | Simple Past | Imperfect | Future |
|---|---|---|---|---|---|
| 1st person singular | yo (I) | puedo | pude | podía | podré |
| 2nd person singular | tú (you—familiar) | puedes | pudiste | podías | podrás |
| 3rd person singular | él, ella (he, she) usted (you—formal) | puede | pudo | podía | podrá |
| 1st person plural | nosotros (we) nosotras (we) | podemos | pudimos | podíamos | podremos |
| 3rd person plural | ellos, ellas (they) ustedes (you all) | pueden | pudieron | podían | podrán |

## *Querer* (To want, to love)

|  | Subject Pronoun | Present | Simple Past | Imperfect | Future |
|---|---|---|---|---|---|
| 1st person singular | yo (I) | quiero | quise | quería | querré |
| 2nd person singular | tú (you—familiar) | quieres | quisiste | querías | querrás |
| 3rd person singular | él, ella (he, she) usted (you—formal) | quiere | quiso | quería | querrá |
| 1st person plural | nosotros (we) nosotras (we) | queremos | quisimos | queríamos | querremos |
| 3rd person plural | ellos, ellas (they) ustedes (you all) | quieren | quisieron | querían | querrán |

## *Saber* (To know)

|  | Subject Pronoun | Present | Simple Past | Imperfect | Future |
|---|---|---|---|---|---|
| 1st person singular | yo (I) | sé | supe | sabía | sabré |
| 2nd person singular | tú (you—familiar) | sabes | supiste | sabías | sabrás |
| 3rd person singular | él, ella (he, she) usted (you—formal) | sabe | supo | sabía | sabrá |
| 1st person plural | nosotros (we) nosotras (we) | sabemos | supimos | sabíamos | sabremos |
| 3rd person plural | ellos, ellas (they) ustedes (you all) | saben | supieron | sabían | sabrán |

*Tener* (To have)

|  | Subject Pronoun | Present | Simple Past | Imperfect | Future |
|---|---|---|---|---|---|
| 1st person singular | yo (I) | tengo | tuve | tenía | tendré |
| 2nd person singular | tú (you—familiar) | tienes | tuviste | tenías | tendrás |
| 3rd person singular | él, ella (he, she) usted (you—formal) | tiene | tuvo | tenía | tendrá |
| 1st person plural | nosotros (we) nosotras (we) | tenemos | tuvimos | teníamos | tendremos |
| 3rd person plural | ellos, ellas (they) ustedes (you all) | tienen | tuvieron | tenían | tendrán |

*Venir* (To come)

|  | Subject Pronoun | Present | Simple Past | Imperfect | Future |
|---|---|---|---|---|---|
| 1st person singular | yo (I) | vengo | vine | venía | vendré |
| 2nd person singular | tú (you—familiar) | vienes | viniste | venías | vendrás |
| 3rd person singular | él, ella (he, she) usted (you—formal) | viene | vino | venía | vendrá |
| 1st person plural | nosotros (we) nosotras (we) | venimos | venimos | veníamos | vendremos |
| 3rd person plural | ellos, ellas (they) ustedes (you all) | vienen | vinieron | venían | vendrán |

## *Ver* (to see)

| | Subject Pronoun | Present | Simple Past | Imperfect | Future |
|---|---|---|---|---|---|
| 1st person singular | yo (I) | veo | vi | veía | veré |
| 2nd person singular | tú (you—fam.) | ves | viste | veías | verás |
| 3rd person singular | él, ella (he, she) usted (you—form.) | ve | vio | veía | verá |
| 1st person plural | nosotros (we) nosotras (we) | vemos | vimos | veíamos | veremos |
| 3rd person plural | ellos, ellas (they) ustedes (you all) | ven | vieron | veían | verán |

## COMPOUND TENSES

The present perfect tense in English is formed by using the verb *to have* and a past participle:

> He has eaten.
> We have arrived.

In Spanish the present perfect tense is formed by using the present tense of the verb *haber*. (The pluperfect, discussed later, is formed by using the imperfect tense of the verb *haber*.)

The verb *haber* is conjugated as follows:

### Haber

| | Subject Pronoun | Present | Imperfect |
|---|---|---|---|
| **1st person singular** | yo (I) | he | había |
| **2nd person singular** | tú (you—familiar) | has | habías |
| **3rd person singular** | él, ella (he, she) usted (you—formal) | ha | había |
| **1st person plural** | nosotros (we) nosotras (we) | hemos | habíamos |
| **3rd person plural** | ellos, ellas (they) ustedes (you all) | han | habían |

Thus:

> *Ha comido.* (He has eaten.)
> *Hemos llegado.* (We have arrived.)

The words *comido* (eaten) and *llegado* (arrived) in the above sentences are the past participles. Regular past participles are formed as follows:
With -*ar* verbs, replace the *ar* with *ado*.
With -*er* and -*ir* verbs, replace the *er* or *ir* with *ido*.

| | |
|---|---|
| hablar | *hablado* |
| comer | *comido* |
| vivir | *vivido* |

However, there are a number of irregular past participles:

| | |
|---|---|
| *hacer* (to do, to make) | *hecho* (made) |
| *decir* (to say) | *dicho* (said) |
| *escribir* (to write) | *escrito* (written) |
| *morir* (to die) | *muerto* (died) |
| *poner* (to put) | *puesto* (put) |
| *romper* (to break, crack, tear) | *roto* (broken) |
| *ver* (to see) | *visto* (seen) |
| *volver* (to return) | *vuelto* (returned) |

### Uses of the present perfect

In Latin America, the present perfect is used much as it is used in English. Although the present perfect tense refers to a past action, it has the feeling of a present state.

> *¿Quieres comer?* (Do you want to eat?)
> *No, he comido.* (No, I've eaten. [I am in the present state of having eaten.])
> *¿Cuándo comiste?* (When did you eat?)
> *Comí hace una hora.* (I ate an hour ago.)

Or,

> *¿Quieres ver esa película?* (Do you want to see that film?)
> *No, la he visto.* (No, I have seen it. [I am in the present state of having seen it.])
> *¿Cuándo?* (When?)
> *La vi ayer.* (I saw it yesterday.)

In general, if the use of the present perfect feels right in English, it is probably OK in Spanish.

Note: In Spain the present perfect is used much more extensively, particularly in spoken Spanish. Since this book focuses on Latin American Spanish, we won't concern ourselves with this practice.

## The pluperfect

Beginners in Spanish probably won't use the pluperfect (also called the past perfect) much. The pluperfect is formed using the imperfect of *haber* and the past participle. Again, it is used much as it is in English. Here is an example:

*Cuando llegamos, ya habían salido.* (When we arrived, they had already gone out.)

### CONTINUOUS FORMS

The continuous tense of verbs, sometimes called the progressive tense, is formed with *estar* and the present participle:

*Estoy hablando.* (I am talking.)
*Estábamos comiendo.* (We were eating.)

The words *hablando* (talking) and *comiendo* (eating) in the above sentences are the present participles. Regular present participles are formed as follows:
With *-ar* verbs, replace the *ar* with *ando*.
With *-er* and *-ir* verbs, replace the *er* or *ir* with *iendo*.

| | |
|---|---|
| *hablar* | *hablando* |
| *comer* | *comiendo* |
| *vivir* | *viviendo* |

However, there are a number of irregular past participles (though they are not very irregular). Here are some of the more common ones:

| | |
|---|---|
| *decir* (to say) | *diciendo* (saying) |
| *dormir* (to sleep) | *durmiendo* (sleeping) |
| *ir* (to go) | *yendo* (going) |
| *pedir* (to ask for) | *pidiendo* (asking for) |
| *venir* (to come) | *viniendo* (coming) |

### Uses

Spanish does not use the continuous form as often as English does. Keep in mind two simple guidelines:
1. The continuous form is almost never used with verbs of motion.

*Llegamos ahora.* (We are arriving now.) (Not: *Estamos llegando ahora.*)

2. The continuous form requires that the action actually be going on.

*Estoy hablando.* (I am talking. [Right now.])

This is different from English, which can use the continuous to speak of both habitual and future actions.

Where English says: What are you doing tonight? I'm studying.
Spanish says: *¿Qué haces esta noche? Voy a estudiar.*

Where English says: I'm running a lot these days.
Spanish says: *Corro mucho estos días.*

There is a bit more to say about this, but if you follow these two rules, you will not go too far astray.

## TO BE OR NOT TO BE (*SER, ESTAR*)

Spanish has several ways of saying *to be*; let us begin with *ser* and *estar*. Both are irregular verbs. Here is how they are conjugated.

### *Ser* (To be)

| | Subject Pronoun | Present | Simple Past | Imperfect | Future |
|---|---|---|---|---|---|
| 1st person singular | yo (I) | soy | fui | era | seré |
| 2nd person singular | tú (you—familiar) | eres | fuiste | eras | serás |
| 3rd person singular | él, ella (he, she) usted (you—formal) | es | fue | era | será |
| 1st person plural | nosotros (we) nosotras (we) | somos | fuimos | éramos | seremos |
| 3rd person plural | ellos, ellas (they) ustedes (you all) | son | fueron | eran | serán |

### *Estar* (To be)

| | Subject Pronoun | Present | Simple Past | Imperfect | Future |
|---|---|---|---|---|---|
| 1st person singular | yo (I) | estoy | estuve | estaba | estaré |
| 2nd person singular | tú (you—familiar) | estás | estuviste | estabas | estarás |
| 3rd person singular | él, ella (he, she) usted (you—formal) | está | estuvo | estaba | estará |
| 1st person plural | nosotros (we) nosotras (we) | estamos | estuvimos | estábamos | estaremos |
| 3rd person plural | ellos, ellas (they) ustedes (you all) | están | estuvieron | estaban | estarán |

### When to use *ser* and when to use *estar*

The simplest way to remember which is which is this:

*Ser* refers to essence; *estar* refers to state.

In fact, the past participle of *estar*, *estado*, means *state*. Here are some examples of how *ser* and *estar* are used:

*Soy americano, pero estoy en Bolivia.* (I'm an American, but I am in Bolivia.)

*Soy* is used for *americano* because that is part of what defines me, my essence, my identity. However, at the moment, I am in Bolivia. (In general, locations require *estar*, even if they seem permanent.) Notice the change in meaning in the following:

*Es callado.* (He is a quiet person.)
*Está callado.* (He is being quiet.)

The first refers to the essence of the person and the second to a state that the person is in now. Since *ser* refers to the essence of a person or thing, it tends to be more permanent. However, some states can also be permanent and yet still be states. The most dramatic example of this is *está muerto* (he is dead). A state can be an emotional state or a physical state.

*Estoy contento.* (I am happy.)
*¿Estás lista?* (Are you ready?)

### Location

*Estar* is used for the location of an object.

*La mesa está en la cocina.* (The table is in the kitchen.)
*Mi casa está en Boston.* (My house is in Boston.)

This is because the location of an object is not considered to be part of its essence. The only exception to using *estar* with location is that *ser* is used with the location of an event (rather than a thing) since the location of an event is considered part of its essence, unlike the location of a physical object, which could be uprooted and moved. Well, that's the theory, anyway.

*La fiesta de cumpleaños es en mi casa.* (The birthday party is at my house.)
*Mi casa está en la calle Baker.* (My house is on Baker street.)

## Time

*Ser* is used for expressing the time:

> *¿Qué hora es?* (What time is it?)
> *Son las cuatro.* (It is four.)

(See "Time" in this grammar guide for more details on telling time.)

## Impersonal expressions

*Ser* is used for most impersonal expressions. Impersonal expressions are those whose subject is "it."

> *Es importante pensar.* (It is important to think.)
> *Es verdad que vine.* (It is true that I came.)

## Possession

*Ser* is used for possession or ownership.

> *El libro es de Juan.* (The book is Juan's.)
> *El coche es mío.* (The car is mine.)

## Some exceptions

Usually *estar* is used for a state of mind, such as happiness or sadness.

> *Estoy bien.* (I am well.)
> *Está contento.* (He is happy.)
> *Están tristes.* (They are sad.)

However, there are some exceptions. For example, *feliz* frequently takes *ser* even though it refers to a state.

> *Soy feliz ahora.* (I am happy now.)

There is no real explanation for this. Other exceptions include *pobre* (poor) and *rico* (rich) and a few others.

> *Es muy pobre.* (He is very poor.)

## TO BE OR NOT TO BE (*TENER, HAY*)

### *Tener*

Many expressions that use *to be* in English use *tener* (to have) in Spanish. (*Tener* is conjugated under "Irregular Verbs" above.) These include:

*tener hambre* (to be hungry)
*tener sed* (to be thirsty)
*tener calor* (to be hot)
*tener frío* (to be cold)
*tener razón* (to be right)
*tener cuidado* (to be careful)
*tener celos* (to be jealous)
*tener sueño* (to be sleepy)
*tener suerte* (to be lucky)
*tener prisa* (to be in a hurry)
*tener éxito* (to be successful)

In these cases, the words *hambre, sed, calor,* etc. are nouns—one "has hunger." Therefore, you would use the adjective *mucho* (*mucha, muchos, muchas*) in these expressions rather than the adverb *muy.*

Here are some sentences:

*Tengo hambre.* (I am hungry.)
*Tengo mucha hambre.* (I am very hungry.)
*¿Tienes sueño?* (Are you sleepy?)
*Tiene muchos celos de su hermana.* (He is very jealous of his sister.)
*Tengo miedo de los ratones.* (I am afraid of mice.)

*Tener* is also used for age.

*¿Cuántos años tienes?* (How old are you?)
*Tengo siete años.* (I am seven years old.)

One important idiomatic use of *tener* (although not related to the English verb *to be*) is to show obligation. For this we use *tener que.*

*Tiene que ir al médico.* (He has to go to the doctor.)
*Tengo muchas cosas que hacer.* (I have many things to do.)

### *Hay* (and *estar*)

*Hay* means *there is* or *there are*. (Note that this is an anomaly in Spanish, a single form being used for both singular and plural.)

> *Hay un lápiz en la caja.* (There is a pencil in the box.)
> *Hay dos gatos en mi casa.* (There are two cats at my house.)

In the past tense, *there was* and *there were* are translated as *había*.

> *Había un lápiz en la caja.* (There was a pencil in the box.)
> *Había dos gatos en mi casa.* (There were two cats at my house.)

However, when *there* refers to a location, then you will usually use *estar*.

> *Los lápices están allí.* (The pencils are there.)

## COMMANDS

Commands are sentences or phrases that tell someone what to do or what not to do. As you can imagine, this situation arises a lot with children. In what follows we give you the command forms of verbs. However, you can almost always avoid the command forms. At the end of this lesson we show you how.

### Telling children to do something

The commands you would use to address one child in Spanish have different forms in the affirmative (telling her to do something) and the negative (telling her not to do something). For regular verbs, these singular familiar commands, the forms you will use when telling her to do something, are formed simply by dropping the *s* off of the *tú* form of the present tense. The negative commands, however, are a bit more complicated. The present tense verb endings are first dropped. Then, in the case of *-ar* verbs, the *-er/-ir* present tense ending is added, and in the case of *-er/-ir* verbs, the *-ar* present tense ending is added:

| Verb | Affirmative Singular Command (Familiar) | Negative Singular Command (Familiar) |
|---|---|---|
| Hablar (to speak) | Habla (Speak) | No hables (Don't speak) |
| Comer (to eat) | Come (Eat) | No comas (Don't eat) |
| Escribir (to write) | Escribe (Write) | No escribas (Don't write) |

For regular verbs, the plural commands follow this same, ending-switching pattern in both affirmative and negative (both forms are identical), and, in Latin American Spanish, the one plural form works for both formal and familiar situations:

| Verb | Affirmative Plural Command (Familiar or Formal) | Negative Plural Command (Familiar or Formal) |
|---|---|---|
| Hablar (to speak) | Hablen (Speak) | No hablen (Don't speak) |
| Comer (to eat) | Coman (Eat) | No coman (Don't eat) |
| Escribir (to write) | Escriban (Write) | No escriban (Don't write) |

Note that the forms in the first table are used for talking to one child. The second table forms are used when addressing two or more children.

There are a number of verbs that have irregular command forms. Here are some common ones:

| Verb | Affirmative Singular Commands (Familiar) | Negative Singular Commands (Familiar) |
|---|---|---|
| Ir (to go) | Ve (Go) | No vayas (Don't go) |
| Venir (to come) | Ven (Come) | No vengas (Don't come) |
| Decir (to say) | Di (Say) | No digas (Don't say) |
| Hacer (to do, make) | Haz (Do/Make) | No hagas (Don't do/make) |
| Poner (to put) | Pon (Put) | No pongas (Don't put) |

Here are their plural forms. Note that they are the same in affirmative and negative:

| Verb | Affirmative Plural Commands (Familiar or Formal) | Negative Plural Commands (Familiar or Formal) |
|---|---|---|
| Ir (to go) | Vayan (Go) | No vayan (Don't go) |
| Venir (to come) | Vengan (Come) | No vengan (Don't come) |
| Decir (to say) | Digan (Say) | No digan (Don't say) |
| Hacer (to do, make) | Hagan (Do/Make) | No hagan (Don't do/make) |
| Poner (to put) | Pongan (Put) | No pongan (Don't put) |

### Object pronouns with commands

1. We saw in the lesson on object pronouns that they generally precede the verb. Following this general rule, in negative commands place object pronouns before the verb. They are not an exception.

*¡No me digas!* (Don't tell me!)
*No me lo des.* (Don't give me it.)
*No lo hagas rápido.* (Don't do it quickly.)
*No me lo cuentes.* (Don't tell me about it.)

Affirmative commands are an important exception, however. Attach object pronouns to the end of positive commands.

*Dime!* (Tell me!)
*Dámelo.* (Give me it.)
*Hazlo rápido.* (Do it quickly.)
*Cuéntamelo.* (Tell me about it.)

## Other ways of indicating commands

One can almost always avoid using one of the above command forms by saying it in a different way.

### USE *QUERER.*

*¿Me lo quieres hacer?* (Will you do it for me?)
*¿Quieres comer tu carne?* (Will you eat your meat?)
*Quieres hacerlo ahora?* (Will you do it now?)

### USE *DEBER.*

*No debes hacerlo.* (You must not do it.)
*Debes recoger los juguetes.* (You must pick up your toys.)

### USE A FORM OF *IR A* IN THE PRESENT TENSE AND THE INFINITIVE.

*Vas a ir a la cama ahora.* (You are going to bed now.)
*No vas a pegarle a tu hermanito.* (You are not going to hit your little brother.)

### USE *ES HORA DE.*

*Es hora de ir a la cama.* (It is time to go to bed.)
*Es hora de cepillarte los dientes.* (It is time to brush your teeth.)

## PRONOMINAL VERBS

Pronominal verbs, often called reflexive verbs, have objects that are the same as the subject of the verb. For example,

> *Me lavo.* (I wash myself.)
> *Me acuesto.* (I put myself to bed [I go to bed].)
> *Se llama Juan.* (He calls himself Juan [His name is Juan].)

Spanish uses pronominal verbs a lot more than English does. We cannot go into all of the uses of pronominal verbs, but here are some examples of their uses:

### Doing unto oneself and to others

Many verbs in Spanish have a nonpronominal form and a pronominal form. The first refers to actions done to someone or something else, the second to actions done to oneself.

> *bañar, bañarse*
> *Bañé a mi perro.* (I bathed my dog.)
> *Me bañé.* (I bathed. [I took a bath.])

> *despertar, despertarse*
> *Despertamos a los niños.* (We woke up the kids.)
> *Nos despertamos.* (We woke up.)

Notice that in English one does not have to say *I bathed myself.* Rather, one can say *I bathed.* In Spanish, one has to use the pronominal form. (Simply saying *bañé* doesn't work.) This use can apply to inanimate subjects as well.

> *abrir, abrirse*
> *Abrí la puerta.* (I opened the door.)
> *La puerta se abrió.* (The door opened.)

Again, the pronominal form (*La puerta se abrió*) is mandatory to convey the meaning of the second sentence above, even though the door did not really open itself. The sentence *La puerta abrió* would not make sense to a Spanish speaker.

## Changing meaning

In some cases, the pronominal form has a slightly, or significantly, different meaning.

> *dormir* (to sleep), *dormirse* (to fall asleep)
> *Durmieron mucho.* (They slept a lot.)
> *Se durmieron rápido.* (They fell asleep quickly.)

One important case that you will see a lot:

> *ir* (to go), *irse* (to go away, to leave)
> *Me voy.* (I'm leaving.)
> *Vete.* (Leave. Go away. Get out of here. [Note the command form.])
> *Voy a la casa de Roberto.* (I am going to Robert's house.)

## Use in place of possessive adjectives

Spanish does not like to use possessive forms with parts of the body or clothing. Instead, it will use a pronominal form of the verb, or an indirect object if the action applies to someone other than the subject.

> *Tienes que cepillarte los dientes.* (You have to brush your teeth.)
> *¿Te has lavado las manos?* (Have you washed your hands?)
> *Voy a lavarte las manos.* (I am going to wash your hands.)

Note that if you are doing something *with* a part of your body, rather than *to* a part of your body, Spanish will not generally use a pronoun.

> *Lávate las manos.* (Wash your hands.)
> *Levanta la mano si quieres hablar.* (Raise your hand if you want to speak.)

In other words, if it takes one part of your body to do it to another part of your body, it's probably reflexive. If this makes sense, great! If not, don't worry about it.

### The passive voice

The pronominal form can also be used to express the passive voice. In this type of sentence, we are not interested in who is performing the action.

*Eso no se hace.* (That is not done.)
*Se habla español aquí.* (Spanish is spoken here.)
*Se venden libros infantiles allí.* (Children's books are sold there.)

## FORMING NEGATIVES

Negative statements are formed by putting a negative word into the statement. Most often that word is a *no*. The *no* precedes the verb. If pronouns precede the verb, the *no* goes before them. (One never separates pronouns from their verbs.)

> *No habla español.* (He doesn't speak Spanish.)
> *No lo escribí.* (I did not write it.)
> *No voy a hacerlo.* (I am not going to do it.)

There are other negative words. These include:

> *nada* (nothing)
> *nadie* (no one)
> *ni . . . ni* (neither . . . nor)
> *ninguno* (none, no)
> *nunca* (never)
> *jamás* (never)
> *apenas* (hardly)
> *en absoluto* (absolutely not)
> *tampoco* (nor)

These can appear before the verb or after it. If they appear after it, a *no* appears before the verb also, forming a double negative. (English does not like double negatives; Spanish requires them in these situations.)

> *Nadie lo dijo.* (No one said it.) [or *No lo dijo nadie.*]
> *No dije nada.* (I said nothing.)
> *Ni Juan ni Elena puede hacerlo.* (Neither Juan nor Elena can do it.)
> *Tampoco puedo hacerlo.* (Nor can I do it.)
> *No lo hace nunca.* (She never does it.)
> *No conozco a nadie.* (I don't know anybody.)

Note the following:

1. *Ninguno* can be either a pronoun or an adjective. As a pronoun it has the same gender as the noun it is replacing. As an adjective it has the same gender as the noun that it modifies. As an adjective, if it comes before and modifies a masculine noun, it drops the *-o* (and adds an accent).

*No voy a comprar ningún coche ahora.* (I am not going to buy any car now.)
*No voy a comprar ninguna casa ahora.* (I am not going to buy any
house now.)
*Ninguno de los hombres podía leer.* (None of the men could read.)
*Ninguna de ellas vino.* (None of them came [referring to women or girls].)

2. *Nunca* is used more often than *jamás*. *Jamás* is stronger. *Nunca jamás* is very strong.

*No voy a hacerlo nunca jamás.* (I am not going to do it ever.)

3. As in English, *apenas* (hardly) is a negative.

*Apenas te conozco.* (I hardly know you.)
*No te conozco apenas.* (I hardly know you.)

4. Note that *en absoluto* means the opposite of what you might intuit.

*¿Vas a llamarlo?* (Are you going to call him?)
*¡En absoluto!* (Absolutely not!)

## ASKING QUESTIONS

Many questions are formed simply by changing the inflection of the voice.

*Habla español.* (She speaks Spanish.)
*¿Habla español?* (Does she speak Spanish?)

Questions can be formed by inverting the subject and object order:

*¿Habla Ana español?*

Other questions are formed using interrogatory words such as:

*¿quién?* (who?)
*¿qué?* (what?)
*¿cuándo?* (when?)
*¿dónde?* (where?)
*¿por qué?* (why?)
*¿para qué?* (what for?)
*¿cuánto?* (how much, how many?)
*¿cuál?* (which)

Note the following:
1. When a question is introduced by one of these words, the subject, if expressed, follows the verb.

*¿Qué hace ella?* (What does she do?)
*¿Cuándo va Alicia al dentista?* (When does Alicia go to the dentist?)

2. All of these interrogatives have written accents. These do not affect the pronunciation but serve to distinguish these words from conjunctions.

*¿Cuándo te vas?* (When are you leaving?)
*Me voy cuando estés lista.* (I'll leave when you are ready.)

### Cuál or qué

Generally speaking, *qué* means *what* and *cuál* means *which*. As in English, both can be used as pronouns or as adjectives. However, Spanish uses these differently than English. Here are some simple rules:

1. *Qué* is almost always the choice for use as an adjective.

*¿Qué casa es la nuestra?* (Which house is ours?)

2. *Cuál* is often the choice for use as a pronoun. This is because you are being asked to choose among various discrete possibilities.

*¿Cuál es el problema?* (What is the problem?)
*¿Cuál es tu dirección?* (What is your address?)
*¿Cuál quieres?* (Which do you want?)

3. *Qué* can be used as a pronoun if the question is more open-ended or if the question is definitional.

*¿Qué es eso?* (What is that?)
*¿Qué es la felicidad?* (What is happiness?)
*¿Qué quieres comer?* (What do you want to eat?)
*¿Qué quieres?* (What do you want?)

Again, understanding this usage will come with time. You will get a feel for it as you use the phrases in this book.

## POR AND PARA

### The general notion

Both *por* and *para* are roughly translated as *for* but are often used in other situations as well. English speakers often have difficulty knowing which to employ. Here is the general principle:

*Para* looks forward to the goal or result.

*Estudio para el examen.* (I am studying for the exam.)
*Se preparó para nadar.* (He prepared himself to swim.)

*Por* looks back at the cause or reason.

*No fuimos por la nieve.* (We didn't go because of the snow.)
*La amo por su amabilidad.* (I love her for [because of] her kindness.)

### Uses of *para*

Again, the general rule is that *para* looks forward to the goal or result.

*Vamos para la iglesia.* (We are going to the church.) [In this context *para* could be substituted by *a*.]
*Este regalo es para tí.* (This gift is for you.)
*Estará listo para las diez.* (It will be ready by ten.)
*Comer demasiado no es bueno para la salud.* (Eating too much is not good for your health.)
*Todo mi amor es para ti.* (All my love is for you.)

Here are some other uses of *para* that may be less obvious:

*Para* is used to give a reaction or impression.

*Para mí, no es importante.* (For me, it is not important.)

*Para* is used in the following expressions, meaning "considering":

*Es pequeño para su edad.* (He is small for his age. He is small considering his age.)

*Para* can mean "on the point of."

> *La comida estaba para quemarse.* (The food was on the point of burning.)

### Uses of *por*

Again, *por* looks back at the cause or reason.

> *No podía dormir por el calor.* (I couldn't sleep because of the heat.)
> *Sufre por su enfermedad.* (He suffers because of his illness.)

Note that one says

> *Gracias por el regalo.* (Thanks for the gift.)

(One is giving thanks because of the gift, not in order to get it.)

*Por* is used for exchanges.

> *Lo vendió por tres dólares.* (He sold it for three dollars.)
> *¿Puedes darme seis huevos por esta harina?* (Can you give me six eggs for this flour?)

When talking about work, *por* and *para* can indicate different circumstances:

> *Trabajo para el Señor Hernández.* (I work for Mr. Hernández. [He is my employer.])
> *Trabajo por el Señor Hernández.* (I am working for Mr. Hernández. [I am substituting for him. Perhaps he is sick.])

*Por* is used to show support.

> *Votaron por él.* (They voted for him.)
> *Estoy por combatir la pobreza.* (I am for combating poverty.)
> *Come por dos.* (She is eating for two.)

*Por* is used to indicate the agent in a passive construction.

> *La casa fue construida por Saraí.* (The house was built by Saraí.)

When used with location, por means *around, by, through, throughout,* and the like. (By contrast, *para* indicates a goal or destination.)

> *Pasamos por la iglesia.* (We passed by the church. We stopped in at the church.)
> *Vamos a viajar por España.* (We are going to travel through Spain.)
> *Entró por la ventana.* (She entered through the window.)
> *Está por aquí.* (It's around here.)

> *Por* is used in some common idiomatic phrases.

> *Por lo visto, no quiere comer.* (Apparently, he doesn't want to eat.)
> *Vamos a hacerlo, por si acaso.* (Let's do it, just in case.)

As with all these grammar lessons, there is more to say about *por* and *para,* but the above will cover the vast majority of cases.

## TIME

Spanish speakers express the notion of time in a variety of ways. The most common expressions involve the words *tiempo*, *vez*, and *hora*.

### Hora

*Hora* refers to time of day. Let's start with some common expressions for telling time:

*¿Qué hora es?* (What time is it?)
*¿Tienes la hora?* (Do you have the time?)
*Es la una.* (It is one o'clock.)
*Es la una y media.* (It is one-thirty.)
*Son las ocho.* (It is eight o'clock.)

Note: *La* and *las* are used because *hora* is feminine.

Expressions using *y*:

*Son las ocho y diez.* (It is 8:10.)
*Son las ocho y quince.* (It is 8:15.)
*Son las ocho y cuarto.* (It is a quarter past eight.)
*Son las ocho y treinta.* (It is eight-thirty.)
*Son las ocho y media.* (It is half past eight.)
*Son las ocho y cuarenta y cinco.* (It is 8:45.)

Expressions using *menos*:

*Son las nueve menos quince.* (It is fifteen to nine. [Literally: It is nine minus fifteen.])
*Son las nueve menos cuarto.* (It is a quarter to nine. [Literally: It is nine minus a quarter.])

Expressions using *para* (and sometimes *faltar*):

*Es cuarto para las nueve.* (It is a quarter to nine.)
*Son quince para las nueve.* (It is fifteen to nine.)

Expressing *a.m.* and *p.m.*

> *Son las diez de la mañana.* (It is ten a.m.)
> *Son las cinco de la tarde.* (It is five p.m.)
> *Son las diez de la noche.* (It is ten p.m.)

Other responses to *¿Qué hora es?*

> *Es mediodía.* (It is noon.)
> *Es medianoche.* (It is midnight.)
> *Son las cuatro en punto.* (It is exactly four o'clock.)
> *Son las cinco y media, más o menos.* (It is approximately five-thirty.)

*Hora de* is used to say that it is time to do something.

> *Es hora de dormir.* (It is time to sleep.)
> *Es hora de irnos.* (It is time to leave.)

Note the use of *a* in the following expressions.

> *¿A qué hora vamos?* (What time do we go? At what time do we go?)
> *Vamos a las tres.* (We go at three.)
> *¿A qué hora es la fiesta?* (At what time is the party?)
> *La fiesta es a las diez y media.* (The party is at ten thirty.)

### Where's the big hand?

| Where is the big hand? | *¿Dónde está la manecilla grande?* |
| The big hand is on the three. | *La manecilla grande está en el tres.* |
| The big hand is between one and two. | *La manecilla grande está entre el uno y el dos.* |

### Tiempo

*Tiempo* is a time period, a time that endures, even if briefly.

> *¿Cuánto tiempo se tarda en lavar los platos?* (How much time does it take to wash the dishes?)

To spend time is *pasar tiempo*. In addition, there are a number of other ways to indicate that you are spending time being somewhere or doing something.

> *Vamos a pasar un mes en California.* (We are going to spend a month in California.)
> *Vamos a estar en Boston por tres días.* (We are going to be in Boston for three days.)
> *Vamos a pasar tres días esquiando.* (We are going to spend three days skiing.)

If the period of time you are referring to is still ongoing, you can use *llevar.*

> *Llevamos mucho tiempo aquí.* (We have been here for a long time.)

Note: *Tiempo* also means weather. This is completely unrelated to its use in expressions of time.

> *¿Qué tiempo hace?* (What is the weather like?)
> *Hace buen tiempo.* (It is nice weather.)

### Vez

*Vez* refers to an instance or instances (*veces*).

> *Lo hice cinco veces.* (I did it five times.)

Here are some common idiomatic expressions using *vez.*

> *A veces me gusta cantar.* (*Sometimes* I like to sing.)
> *Puedo cantar y bailar a la vez.* (I can sing and dance *at the same time.*)
> *Hazlo otra vez.* (Do it *again.*)
> *Muchas veces duerme tarde.* (*Often* she sleeps late.)
> *Raras veces toma café.* (He *rarely* drinks coffee.)
> *Come frijoles en vez de carne.* (He eats beans *instead of* meat.)

### How to say "ago" in Spanish (and similar expressions)

Most of the time you will use *hace* in conjunction with a verb in the preterite tense to say *ago.*

> *Llegué hace dos horas.* (I arrived two hours ago.)
> *Hace dos horas que llegué.* (I arrived two hours ago.)

Note: If you lead with the word *hace* you need to add the word *que*.

If the action continues into the present then you would use the present tense. (And English would no longer use *ago*.) Consider the following expressions.

> *Hace dos años que estudio español.* (I have been studying Spanish for two years.)
> *Hace dos años que no estudio español.* (I haven't studied Spanish for two years.)
> *Estudio español desde hace dos años.* (I have been studying Spanish for two years.)
> *No estudio español desde hace dos años.* (I haven't studied Spanish for two years.)
> *Estudio español desde el verano pasado.* (I have been studying Spanish since last summer.)

Here is how you might ask some questions regarding time:

> *¿Cuánto tiempo hace que trabajas aquí?* (How long have you worked here?)
> *¿Cuánto tiempo hace que trabajaste aquí?* (How long ago did you work here?)
> *¿Desde cuándo estás enfermo? ¿Cuánto tiempo hace que estás enfermo?* (Since when have you been sick? How long have you been sick?)
> *¿Cuándo estuviste enfermo?* (When were you sick?)

A very popular way of expressing action that started in the past and continues now is to use *llevar*.

> *¿Cuánto tiempo llevas aquí?* (How long have you been here?)
> *Llevo tres años aquí.* (I have been here three years.)
> *Llevo meses diciendo eso.* (I have been saying that for months.)

Note that when you use *llevar*, the event must still be going on.

### Now

You probably have learned that the word for *now* is *ahora*, and this is correct.

> *Ahora nos vamos.* (We are leaving now.)
> *Está lloviendo ahora.* (It is raining now.)

Nevertheless, among native Spanish speakers, the most common way to say now is *ya*. Perhaps this comes from the simple exclamatory quality of *ya*! To quote from a well-regarded grammar book, *ya* "can indicate impatience, accumulating frustration, fulfilled expectations, resignation, certainty about the future . . ."[1] (Do any of these ever apply to your interactions with your kids?)

> *Ya está aquí.* (She is here now.)
> *Ya salen.* (They are leaving now.)
> *Hazlo ya, por favor.* (Do it now, please.)
> *Ya es hora.* (It is time.)
> *Ya es hora de irnos.* (It is time for us to go.)

When someone is pouring a drink, you could say:

> *Dime cuando.* (Tell me when [that's enough].)
> *¡Ya!* (Now! [Enough!])

Likewise, if the kids are teasing or fighting, you could say:

> *¡Basta ya!* (Enough now!)

Or simply:

> *¡Ya!*

When used with the past tense, *ya* usually means already.

> *Ya llegaron.* (They already arrived.)

In the negative, *ya* just translates to *no longer.*

> *Ya no trabajan aquí.* (They no longer work here.)

Finally, there are some expressions using *ya* that you might find useful.

> *¡Ya empezamos!* (Here we go again!)
> *Ya, ya . . . y tú no hicisite nada.* (Yeah, sure . . . and you didn't do anything.)

---

1. Butt and Benjamin, *A New Reference Grammar of Modern Spanish*, 2d ed. (Lincolnwood, IL: NTC Publishing Group, 1995), 397.

*Ya que estamos aquí . . .* (Well, since we're here . . . )
*Ya verás.* (You'll see.)

## Again

There are three ways to say *again.*

*Habló otra vez.* (He spoke again.)
*Habló de nuevo.* (He spoke again.)
*Volvió a hablar.* (He spoke again.)

All of these are pretty common. Just choose the one you like best.

## Just

*Acabar de* (followed by the infinitive) is used to convey the idea that you have just done something.

*Acabo de comer.* (I've just eaten.)
*Acabamos de regresar.* (We've just returned.)

Note that *acabar* in these sentences is in the present tense even though the action is in the recent past.

## What day is today?

| | |
|---|---|
| What day is today? | *¿Qué día es hoy?* |
| | *¿A cómo estamos hoy?* |
| Today is Monday. | *Hoy es lunes.* |

The days of the week are:

| | |
|---|---|
| Monday | *el lunes* |
| Tuesday | *el martes* |
| Wednesday | *el miércoles* |
| Thursday | *el jueves* |
| Friday | *el viernes* |

| | |
|---|---|
| Saturday | *el sábado* |
| Sunday | *el domingo* |

## The date

The word for *date* is *la fecha*.

| | |
|---|---|
| What is the date today? | *¿Cuál es la fecha hoy?* |
| Today is March 14, 2012. | *Hoy es el catorce de marzo de dos mil doce.* |

The months are:

| | |
|---|---|
| January | *enero* |
| February | *febrero* |
| March | *marzo* |
| April | *abril* |
| May | *mayo* |
| June | *junio* |
| July | *julio* |
| August | *agosto* |
| September | *septiembre* |
| October | *octubre* |
| November | *noviembre* |
| December | *diciembre* |

## Yesterday, today, tomorrow

*Mañana* means *tomorrow* and also means *morning*:

| | |
|---|---|
| We are going to the show tomorrow. | *Vamos al espectáculo mañana.* |
| We are going to the park tomorrow morning. | *Vamos al parque mañana por la mañana.* |

Today and yesterday are just *hoy* and *ayer*, respectively.

| | |
|---|---|
| Today we are going to stay home. | *Hoy nos vamos a quedar en casa.* |
| Yesterday we went to pick apples. | *Ayer fuimos a recoger manzanas.* |

### Next week, last week

| | |
|---|---|
| We did it last Friday. | *Lo hicimos el viernes pasado.* |
| We are going to go next Monday. | *Vamos a ir el lunes que viene.* |
| We are going to visit Grandma and Grandpa a week from Tuesday. | *Vamos a visitar a los abuelos de este martes en ocho.* |
| We go to the play two weeks from Wednesday. | *Vamos a la obra de este miércoles en quince días.* |
| We saw them three weeks ago. | *Los vimos hace tres semanas.* |
| | *Hace tres semanas que los vimos.* |
| We have to return the book to the library within two weeks. | *Tenemos que devolver el libro a la biblioteca dentro de dos semanas.* |

# SPANISH LANGUAGE RESOURCES

## WHAT IS OUT THERE

One great thing about Spanish is that, because it is spoken by about 400 million people worldwide, most people in the United States have easy access to a wealth of books, CDs, MP3s, computer programs, and movies in the language. In what follows, we give a small sampling of what is out there (many of these are materials we have used ourselves). The selection of materials is constantly growing, however, so we will also provide you with some simple suggestions on how to find materials that suit your child's interests or your own.

Although age appropriateness is probably the first thing that comes to a parent's mind when searching out materials, there is a less obvious factor you may want to consider. Film and literature are capable of transmitting, in ways both direct and subtle, the ideals and customs of the culture from which they spring. Works—books, music, and films—originally written in Spanish are more like to convey a sense of the values and aspirations of the society, or segment of society, with which the author is associated. In addition, such materials may capture the day-to-day rhythms of life in other places, giving the audience a sense of cultural notions, often hidden to casual observers, that differ greatly from those held in their own culture. A good work of fiction can reveal deeply held notions about concepts such as beauty, social responsibility, death, marriage, family life, or religion. As outlined at the beginning of this book, we consider the ability to view the world from myriad perspectives to be one of the major benefits of acquiring a second language.

Having acknowledged the importance of experiencing works that originated in Spanish-speaking societies, you may wonder why in the lists that follow there is a preponderance of materials that are, in fact, translations into Spanish. There are some "real-world" factors that come into play when choosing books and movies. Access is one of these. When we first began raising our children bilingually, Spanish-language materials that were not translations could be difficult to find. Fortunately, this has changed dramatically in recent years, so this should be much less of a problem for parents today. However, you may find yourself addressing another recent phenomenon. We refer to the "mega-bestseller." The wildly successful commercialization of books, music, and film—à la *Harry Potter*—often creates a desire, in both kids and adults, to read what everyone else is reading. It has often been affirmed that these books have rekindled a waning desire to read in kids and adolescents. If this is true, this is undoubtedly a positive thing, and if it is true of your child in particular you should not hesitate to exploit "the buzz" that has piqued his or her curiosity. Our kids have read many of these popular books—such as the *Rainbow Fish* stories, the *Harry Potter* series and *Stellaluna*—in Spanish, and they love to tell their friends, "Oh yeah, that was great. I read it in Spanish," and discuss some of the curious differences between the versions (often in the names of characters, things, or places).

Our kids have also watched an endless stream of popular movies in translation. When it comes to finding original-language options in Spanish, however, movies are another matter. In our experience, although many Spanish-speaking countries produce first-rate cinema—often, in our estimation, superior to our own—children's films are conspicuously in short supply. This is one area in which the U.S. industry has dominated, and children growing up in Spanish-speaking societies are quite familiar with American kids' movies. Still, there are some good options out there, and more are being produced every year. It will simply take more searching to find them.

### BOOKS

*El parque prohibido* by Andrés Ibánez (Editorial Montena). A tale that explores the relationship between father and son, as well as the notion of friendship in general.

*Memorias de una gallina*, by Concha López Narváez (Editorial Anaya). The memoirs of a very special hen.

*Un duende a rayas* and *Abuelita Opalina*, by María Puncel (Editorial SM). Charming stories from this prize-winning author of children's literature.

*Historia de ninguno,* by Pilar Mateos (Editorial SM). The adventures of a child so small that nobody notices his presence, by another prize-winning Spanish author of children's literature.

*Ojo de nube,* by Ricardo Gómez Gil. Magical tribal legends.

*Don Quijote cabalga entre versos,* by Antonio Gómez Yebra (Lectorum Publications). The adventures of this most famous knight, in verse.

*Selim, el vendedor de alegría,* by J. Cervon and A. Canas (Editorial Bruño). A popular tale from this Spanish author (Cervon) and illustrator (Canas).

*Aventuras de una rebanada de pizza,* by Ana Luisa Anza (Advanced Marketing). When a cockroach is found on a customer's pizza and the pizza parlor is in danger of shutting down, Irene and her friends team up to solve the mystery and save the pizza parlor.

*Saltando por el bosque,* by Adela Basch (Colección Rehilete). Rabbits in a forest discover a butterfly. Can they accept her even though she is different?

*Cuentos para 365 días,* by Gloria Fuertes (Lectorum Publications). Everything by this well-known Spanish poet and author is excellent and full of humor, warmth, and wit (though not all her work is for children). See the entry under "A Few Websites Showcasing Suggested Authors Writing in Spanish" below.

*The Fish in the Sea (El pez en el mar),* illustrated by Lorella Rizzatti (Ediciones Gaviota). A colorful cardboard picture book for infants. This is part of a series.

*Goodnight Moon (Buenas noches, luna),* by Margaret Wise Brown (Harper Festival/Harper Collins). An all-time favorite cardboard picture book.

*Are You My Mother? (¿Eres tú mi mamá?),* by P. D. Eastman (Random House). A nice book for younger kids.

*Abuela,* by Arthur Dorros, illustrated by Elisa Kleven (Demco Media). A little girl imagines that she is flying around the city with her grandmother. Beautifully illustrated.

*The Little Prince (El Principito),* by Antoine de Saint Exupéry (Harcourt). Written originally in French, this classic has been translated into many languages, including Spanish.

*Six Foolish Fishermen (Seis pescadores disparatados),* recounted by Benjamin Elkin, illustrations by Katherine Evans (Children's Press). A traditional tale about six brothers who haven't learned to count.

*This House Is Made of Mud (Esta casa está hecha de lodo),* by Ken Buchanan, illustrated by Libba Tracy (Turtleback Books). A bilingual story of a house in the Sonoran desert.

*Madeline,* by Ludwig Bemelmans (Live Oak Media). The story of a little French girl and her friends.

*Where the Wild Things Are (Donde están los monstruos),* by Maurice Sendak (Harper Trophy/Harper Collins). The classic tale of a boy and his imagination.

*Whistle for Willie (Silba por Willie)*, by Ezra Jack Keats (Viking Juvenile). A young boy is determined to learn how to whistle. Also, his *A Snowy Day (Un día de nieve)* (Live Oak Media). A young boy and the delights of a snowfall.

*Curious George (Jorge el Curioso)*, by H. C. Rey (bilingual edition; H.M.H. Books). The incorrigible little monkey.

*Pooh's Corner (El rincón de Puh)*, by A. A. Milne (Santillana USA) and his other stories about that not-quite-there bear, Winnie the Pooh.

*The Giving Tree (El árbol generoso)*, by Shel Silverstein (Lectorum Publications). The tree that gave and gave until it could give no more.

*The Legend of the Bluebonnet (La leyenda de la flor 'El Conejo')*, by Tomie de-Paolo (Castillo de Arena). An old Texas Native American legend with a nice story and beautiful illustrations.

*Stellaluna*, by Janell Cannon (Editorial Juventud). Beautifully illustrated book about a little bat who loses her way but makes friends with a trio of little birds.

*Charlotte's Web (Las telarañas de Carlota)*, by E. B. White (Rayo). This is a great book for kids, and its Spanish translation is no exception. Other E. B. White books, such as *Stuart Little*, have also been translated into Spanish.

*Caps for Sale (Se venden gorras)*, by Esphyr Slobodkina (Rayo). A whimsical tale of caps and monkeys.

*The Desert Is My Mother (El desierto es mi madre)*, by Pat Mora, illustrated by Daniel Lechon (Lorito Books). A nicely illustrated book about a little girl and the desert.

*The Great Kapok Tree (El gran capoquero)*, by Lynne Cherry (Harcourt Brace). A beautifully illustrated book about a tree in the Amazon and its inhabitants.

*Colors (De colores)*, by José Luis Orozco, illustrated by Elisa Kleven (Puffin). A beautifully illustrated collection of Latin American children's songs with music and chords. You can also get the audio CD.

*We're Going on a Bear Hunt (Vamos a cazar un oso)*, a fun story retold by Michael Rosen and illustrated by Helen Oxenbury (Ediciones Ekare). The Spanish translation may be better than the original English.

*The Flute Player (La flautista)*, by Robyn Eversole, illustrated by G. Brian Karas (Scholastic). A nice story, beautifully illustrated.

*Grandmother's Nursery Rhymes (Las nanas de abuelita)*, compiled by Nelly Palacio Jaramillo (Henry Holt & Co.). A collection of South American nursery rhymes.

*The Very Hungry Caterpillar (La oruga muy hambrienta)* and other books by Eric Carle (Philomel). Many of Eric Carle's books with simple, appealing stories and collage illustrations have been translated into Spanish.

*If You Give a Mouse a Cookie (Si le das una galleta a un ratón)*, by Laura Joffe Numeroff, illustrated by Felicia Bond (Rayo). Also available in Spanish: *If You Give a Moose a Muffin.*

*Corduroy*, by Don Freeman (Puffin). The story of a teddy bear who gets lost and eventually finds a home.

*The Rainbow Fish (El pez arco iris)*, by Marcus Pfister (Ediciones Norte-Sur). The colorful fish who learns to share. Also available in Spanish: *Destello, el dinosaurio.*

*Mr. Rabbit and the Lovely Present (El señor conejo y el hermoso regalo)*, by Charlotte Zolotow, illustrated by Maurice Sendak (Harper Collins Children's Books). A kindly rabbit helps a little girl find a present for her mother's birthday.

*Alexander, Who Used to Be Rich Last Sunday (Alexander, que era rico el domingo pasado)*, by Judith Viorst, illustrated by Ray Cruz (Aladdin). Alexander has a dollar. It doesn't last long.

Many of the popular children's book series are available in Spanish:

The *Spot* books, by Eric Hill (various publishers). Almost from day one, kids love the Spot books. Most of the titles are available in Spanish.

*The Magic School Bus (El autobús mágico)*, by Joanna Cole et al. (Scholastic en Español). A popular book on science, translated into Spanish.

The *Ramona* books, by Beverly Cleary (Rayo). The adventures of Ramona Quimby and her sister.

Dr. Seuss books, such as *The Cat in the Hat (El gato ensombrerado)* (Random House). Many of these translations actually manage to capture the rhythm and whimsy of Dr. Seuss.

The *Babar* books (Ediciones Beascoa). Stories of the elephant family based on the works of French authors Jean and Laurent de Brunhoff. Various books follow Babar and his family on vacation, in the city, on the farm, in the house, etc.

*Little Critter*, by Gina and Mercer Mayer (Rayo). This popular kids' series about the daily adventures of Little Critter has been translated into Spanish.

*Clifford*, by Norman Bridwell (Scholastic). The big red dog comes to life in Spanish.

*The Berenstain Bears (Los osos Berenstain)*, by Stan and Jan Berenstain (Tandem Library). The trials and triumphs of the bear family.

*Sesame Street* books (various authors and publishers). Many of these titles have been translated into Spanish. The popular television series translated to print.

Disney Books in Spanish (various authors; Random House, Mouse Works, and other publishers). Large hardcover books include *Aladdin, Bambi, The Lion*

King (*El rey león*), Beauty and the Beast (*La bella y la bestia*), Snow White (*Blancanieves*), 101 Dalmatians (*101 dálmatas*), *The Little Mermaid* (*La sirenita*), and more.

## MUSIC ON CD AND MP3

We have come across a number of useful CDs and MP3s. Some are recordings of songs. Here is just a small sampling of what is available.

Cri-cri. There are lots of recordings by this legendary Mexican singer of children's songs.

José Luis Orozco. Orozco has produced a very nice series of recordings of children's songs in Spanish, ranging from traditional Latin American songs to compositions of his own.

*Sing, Dance, Laugh, and Eat Tacos*. A series of recordings with songs to teach counting, animals, culture, family, weather, days of the week, seasons, etc.

## AUDIOBOOKS—RECORDED STORIES ON CD AND MP3

Many stories are available on CD or MP3. Most are accompanied by printed books that allow kids to follow along. Some widely available titles from various publishers are:

The Three Little Pigs (*Los tres cerditos*)
The Pied Piper (*La flautista*)
Henny Penny (*La gallinita Trula*)
Three Billy Goats (*Tres cabritillos*)
The Wolf and Seven Goats (*El lobo y siete cabritas*)
Ali Baba and the 40 Thieves (*Alí Baba y los 40 ladrones*)
Hansel and Gretel (*Hansel y Gretel*)
Disney: Some Disney stories, such as "Pocahontas," are available in audio versions.

## DVDS

When we first started raising our kids, VHS was the predominant media for viewing movies. In order to get materials in Spanish we would have to load up on tapes during trips to Mexico. Fortunately, the advent of the DVD format has virtually eliminated this problem, as most disks give the viewer a range of language options for both the sound track and subtitles in the setup menu. Your local movie store is now packed with viewing options in Spanish. As we discussed above, however, finding movies for kids originally produced in Spanish can still be a difficult task, though those suitable for adolescents are a bit more common.

Virtually every Disney animated movie is available in Spanish translation, including such popular titles as *The Little Mermaid* (*La sirenita*), *Beauty and the Beast* (*La bella y la bestia*) and *The Lion King* (*El rey león*). Disney also has a series of DVDs featuring the songs from the movies under the title of *Sing Along Songs* (*Canta con nosotros*).

A nicely produced Mexican version of the long-running public television series *Sesame Street* (*Plaza sésamo*) is available. This is not a dubbed version of the original but an original Mexican version with similar, though not identical, characters. It should surprise no one that Barney (the purple dinosaur) also speaks Spanish (in dubbed versions of the originals).

## COMPUTER PROGRAMS

A number of popular computer programs are now available in Spanish. Here are a couple that you might recognize, though new programs are constantly coming out and an Internet search will reveal an excellent selection:

*The Living Book Series.* These programs, popular with both prereaders and readers, can be played in Spanish or English with the flip of a switch. Follow the story and more with a click of the mouse.

*Where in the World Is Carmen Sandiego?* (*¿Dónde está Carmen Sandiego?*) This very popular sleuth-as-geographer program is available in a Spanish-language version.

## WHERE TO GET IT

The titles listed above represent just a small sample of what is available. Bookstores in many regions of the country have a respectable number of titles of kids' books in Spanish. You may even be able to find stores that stock kids' recordings and DVDs in Spanish. Most books that we have purchased have come from bookstores. The advantage of buying from a local bookstore is that you can look at the book before you buy (though, as you will see, some websites supply an impressive amount of online samples). Unfortunately, in some areas bookstores do not seem to stock Spanish titles. And it is not as common to find Spanish language CDs everywhere. Fortunately, there is a wide range of materials available by mail or Internet download. If you have access to the web you can get information on titles immediately. If not, simply call and ask for a catalog.

Here we share a few of our favorite sources:

Although there are many sites for ordering materials, and we list some of them below, most of our readers will already be familiar with Amazon. What you may not realize is that Amazon has a portal dedicated to materials in Spanish and probably has the greatest selection of materials. As of now, there is no direct way to get there from its English-language home page. (We have contacted Amazon about this shortcoming and hope that it is remedied soon.) However, you can simply type into your browser "amazon.com /spanish" (do not capitalize "spanish"), hit enter, and it will take you there (the actual site address is http://www.amazon.com/exec/obidos/tg/browse /-/301731, just in case). On the left-hand side of the page, under "Browse," you will find "Audiolibro en Casete," "Audiolibro en Disco Compacto," and "Infantil y juvenil" (children and adolescents). When you click on any of these links you will be presented with many ways to refine your search. (By the way, once you have purchased a book on CD, it is a simple process to convert it to MP3 format, using iTunes or another program, so that your kids can load it onto their MP3 players.)

Amazon's selection includes translations from English of favorites like *Eragon* and *The Circuit* as well as works originally written in Spanish, such as Laura Esquivel's *Malinche* or the wonderful classic *Don Quijote de la Mancha*. At the top of the "Libros en español" page you will find a link to "Advanced Search." Apart from helping you locate a specific book, audiobook, or DVD, this link will let you specify languages for both the soundtrack and the subtitles of movies. Unfortunately, at present there is no way to distinguish original Spanish-language books and movies from translations in the search. We have contacted Amazon about this shortcoming as well and hope that it is remedied in the future. For now, you will have to peruse the titles in order to find the materials that were originally produced in Spanish.

There are many other sites for books, movies, and music in Spanish. An Internet search will quickly return myriad sources for materials in Spanish, some of which supply a surprising amount of free material online. If you like something online, you may want to buy the physical book for more comfortable bedside reading. Here are some you may want to look into:

http://www.bibliotecasvirtuales.com/biblioteca/literaturainfantil/ (Children's books originally in Spanish.)

http://www.literatura-infantil.com/ (Children's books both in the original Spanish and translation. You can search on this site by the age of your child.)

http://www.bibliotecasvirtuales.com/biblioteca/literaturainfantil/ (Children's stories, fables, and poetry; some contemporary, some traditional, some originally in Spanish, others translated to Spanish. You will also find forums and chat rooms as well as links to other virtual libraries.)

http://www.bibliotecasvirtuales.com/biblioteca/OtrosAutoresdelaLiteratura Universal/esopo/fabulas.asp (Aesop's fables: An online collection of some of these classic shorter works.)

http://www.bibliotecasvirtuales.com/biblioteca/literaturainfantil/fabulas /index.asp (An online sample of fables from a variety of sources.)

http://www.bibliotecasvirtuales.com/biblioteca/literaturainfantil/cuentos clasicos/index.asp (A sample of children's stories from masters like Hans Christian Andersen and the Brothers Grimm.)

http://www.boardsnet.com/catalogo_dvd_infantiles_espanol_01.htm (Principally kids' DVDs.)

http://www.amazon.com/Simple-Spanish-Singalong-Songs-Georgette/dp /0962393061/ref=sr_1_62?ie=UTF8&s=books&qid=1215549398&sr=1-62 (Sing-along songs in Spanish.)

http://bibliotecadigital.ilce.edu.mx/sites/RelatosCampeche/relatos.pdf (A PDF with original stories from Campeche, Mexico.)

http://bibliotecadigital.ilce.edu.mx/sites/colibri/htm/menu.htm (Beautifully illustrated stories online.)

http://ca.geocities.com/el_rincon_de_nora/indice_poemas_infantiles.htm (A good selection of children's poetry, some from major literary figures, such as Federico García Lorca and Juan Ramón Jiménez.)

## A Few Websites Showcasing Suggested Authors Writing in Spanish:

**Gloria Fuertes**: Check out this site about the phenomenal poet and author of both children's and adults' literature. It includes both biography and bibliography:

http://www.gloriafuertes.org/

**Rafael Pombo**: Here you will find biographical information and a good sample of this Colombian poet's work for kids online:

http://www.bibliotecasvirtuales.com/biblioteca/literaturainfantil/Poesia infantil/RafaelPombo/index.asp

**María Elena Walsh**: Despite the last name, María Elena is a well-regarded Argentinian author of children's poetry, songs, and stories. Many of her songs can be purchased for download. Look here for a biography and an excellent sample:
http://www.bibliotecasvirtuales.com/biblioteca/literaturainfantil/contempo raneos/mariaelenawalsh/index.asp

**Carmen Gil Martínez**: A fun website with a bio of this well-published Spanish poet, a bibliography, a good sample of her work, and more:
http://www.poemitas.com/

### Other Internet Sites of Interest

Here is a site that provides interactive riddles in Spanish:
http://omega.ilce.edu.mx:3000/sites/litinf/juegos/htm/1jue-adiv.htm

This is a great educational site with an interactive presentation on dinosaurs:
http://bibliotecadigital.ilce.edu.mx/sites/deinos/index.htm

And another on the environment:
http://bibliotecadigital.ilce.edu.mx/sites/educa/html/menu.htm

This site gives the winner and runners-up for a number of literary contests for books written for kids and adolescents. Always a good bet for a lead:
http://lij-jg.blogspot.com/search/label/Premios

This site provides reading recommendations to parents for their kids:
http://www.colorincolorado.org/leer/infantiles

There is, of course, a wide variety of sources for materials, and there is no reason to limit yourself to any one in particular. We have provided some suggestions to help begin your search, but you may begin simply by entering keywords—such as "literatura infantil," "niños, libros, favoritos" or "cuentos, poesía, adolescentes"—into a search engine, such as Google, in order to search the entire web.

# KID NAMES IN SPANISH

When you are talking to your child in Spanish, you can use the same name that you use in English, you can use the same name but pronounce it as you would in Spanish, or you can use a Spanish version of the child's name. (Sometimes kids like to use their Spanish names when they speak Spanish.) Some names in English have similar corresponding names in Spanish. Others do not. Here are some of the more common names and their Spanish equivalents.

## GIRLS, *NIÑAS*

Alexandra, *Alejandra*
Alice, *Alicia*
Andrea, *Andrea*
Angela, *Ángela, Angélica*
Ann, Anne, *Ana*
Beatrice, *Beatriz*
Carla, *Carla*
Catherine, Katherine, *Katarina, Catalina*
Caroline, *Carolina*
Cecilia, *Cecilia*
Christine, *Cristina*
Claire, *Clara*
Claudia, *Claudia*

Daniela, *Daniela*
Dora, *Dora*
Elizabeth, *Isabel*
Ellen, *Elena*
Elsa, *Elsa*
Emerald, *Esmeralda*
Eve, *Eva*
Flora, *Flor*
Gabriela, *Gabriela*
Grace, *Graciela*
Hilda, *Hilda*
Hortense, *Hortensia*
Jane, *Juana*
Julie, *Julia*

Laura, *Laura*

Linda, *Linda*

Lisa, *Lisa*

Margaret, *Margarita*

Martha, *Marta*

Mary, *María*

Miriam, *Miriam*

Monica, *Mónica*

Olga, *Olga*

Olivia, *Olivia*

Patricia, *Patricia*

Paula, *Paula*

Rachel, *Raquel*

Rose, *Rosa*

Sabrina, *Sabrina*

Sarah, *Sara*

Sarai, *Saraí*

Sonya, *Sonia*

Star, *Estrella*

Susan, *Susana, Azucena*

Stella, *Estela*

Tanya, *Tania*

Theresa, *Teresa*

Victoria, *Victoria*

## BOYS, *NIÑOS*

Abraham, *Abram*

Adam, *Adán*

Albert, *Alberto (Beto)*

Alexander, *Alejandro (Alex)*

Andrew, *Andrés*

Anthony, *Antonio*

Charles, *Carlos*

Daniel, *Daniel*

David, *David*

Edward, *Eduardo (Lalo)*

Ernest, *Ernesto*

Francis (Frank), *Francisco (Paco)*

Frederick, *Federico*

Gabriel, *Gabriel*

George, *Jorge*

Gerard, *Gerardo*

Homer, *Homero*

Hugh, *Hugo*

Humbert, *Umberto (Beto, Berto)*

Isaac, *Isaac*

Jacob, *Jacobo*

James, *Jaime*

Jason, *Jasón*

John, *Juan*

Joseph (Joey), *José (Pepe)*

Jules, *Julio*

Louis, *Luis*

Lucas, *Lucas*

Mark, *Marcos*

Matthew, *Mateo*

Michael, *Miguel*

Noah, *Noé*

Paul, *Pablo*

Peter, *Pedro*

Richard, *Ricardo*

Robert (Bob), *Roberto (Beto, Berto)*

Roger, *Rogelio*

Samuel, *Samuel*

Steven, *Esteban*

William, *Guillermo*

# INDEX / GLOSSARY

Where the gender of a noun is not evident by its ending, we have indicated it with an *m* or *f*. Words in Spanish that begin with a stressed *a* will take a masculine article even if they are feminine, for example, *el agua* (f), *el arte* (f). Where the same noun is used with a masculine article when referring to a male and a feminine article when referring to a female, we indicate this (e.g., guide, *el guía, la guía*).